Learning Leadership from Biblical Leaders: Lessons in Leadership Qualities

Joshua Erin Elliott

DEDICATION

I want to take a moment to thank a few people that helped inspire this book.

First, I want to thank God for giving me the insights and talent to write this book.

I want to thank my Mom and Dad for their belief in me and for bringing me up in a Christian home.

I want to thank my daughter, Madison, for always being there and loving her daddy.

Finally, I want to thank Carla. You have always been there for me even when I was not always there for you. You have never given up on me and that means the world to me. You inspire me to always be my best. Thank you for loving and believing in me.

CONTENTS

ACKNOWLEDGMENTS

Thank you to Joy Elliott for editing and proofing. Thank you to Alyssa Hubbard for helping me and leading me in the right direction for publishing my first book.

INTRODUCTION

I have always wanted to write a book ever since I started studying

and learning more and more about leadership. Being a student of

leadership has made me want to share what I have learned with

others. I have attempted to write books multiple times over the past

years but I would always reach a dead end with the concept. This

past year, I made it a goal to read the Bible in a year. While

reading the Bible, the concept of my book was made clear to me

and thus I began to write the material that I will be sharing with

you in the chapters that follow. God gave me this idea and I hope

that I gave it the justice that it deserves and that it will help you in

your leadership journey. *Learning Leadership from Biblical*

Leaders: Lessons in Leadership Qualities will teach you many

qualities of leadership from biblical leaders. It will teach you lessons that will help make your leadership better. It will also give you insight into how people are called to become leader. While writing this book, I have grown stronger in my faith as well as my leadership. I hope you will find that it does the same for you. Leadership is a journey and we all need guidance and growth to make it through. God has chosen us as leaders and He has given us a roadmap and guide to help us become successful leaders. It is up to us to use it and learn from it. I have used parts of His great book, The Bible, to teach the lessons in the following pages. There are many lessons that I did not use in this book, so I encourage you to learn more after you read this book by reading The Bible. It will strengthen you and guide you. There is no greater leadership book. I hope you enjoy this book and learn from it and that it will strengthen your leadership. Leadership is a journey and I am thankful that I will get to be a small part of your journey. Enjoy *Learning Leadership from Biblical Leaders!*

JOB

Job shows us how commitment can lead us through adversity as leaders.

Job 13:15 (NKJV) says, "Though He slay me, yet will I trust him." Even though Job lost everything in his life, he stayed committed to God. Commitment is a key quality of a leader and we can learn a lot from Job when it comes to this quality. As a leader you must stay committed to the vision, the goals, your followers, and most importantly yourself no matter what comes at you. At times your commitment will be tested as it was with Job, but you have to stand firm and make it through. This is why commitment and adversity go hand in hand. You will face adversity in order to see how committed you are.

Let's start by looking at the definitions for commitment and adversity. These definitions come from *The Merriam-Webster Dictionary*. "Commitment is defined as a promise to do or give something, a promise to be loyal to someone or something, and the attitude of someone who works very hard to do or support something (1)." As we look at this definition, we see that commitment is easily a quality of a leader. Leaders are loyal to their followers and they have the attitude to work very hard and to be supportive.

Adversity is defined as "a difficult situation or condition (2)." As a leader there will be many times that we are faced with difficult situations. How we handle these situations will determine the level of commitment we have as leaders. Some leaders run and hide from adversity and then they fail. Other leaders grab adversity by the "horns" and tackle it straight on in order to grow themselves and their people.

"Job was a man that was blameless and upright and one who feared God and shunned evil (Job 1:1 - NKJV)." But God still allowed him to face adversity to see his commitment to Him. Job lost his wealth, his family, his friends, and ultimately his health, but he never lost his commitment to God. He was tried and tested and most men would have failed and lost their commitment, but Job did not. All leaders can learn from Job the value of commitment in the face of adversity.

How you face adversity will determine your commitment and determines what happens to you as a leader. The following chart shows a few of those items:

Face It Positively:	Face It Negatively:
Strengthen as a Leader	Weaken as a Leader
Followers are encouraged	Followers are discouraged
Momentum builds	Momentum dies
Productivity Increases	Productivity Decreases

Job lost everything he worked for and everything that God had blessed him with including his family and his health; however, Job remained steadfast. Job's friends came to listen and help encourage him in his time of adversity – even though in the end they did the opposite. You need encouragement to overcome adversity. Even a leader needs help to overcome adversity and does not have to do so alone. As a leader do not be afraid to ask for help from those closest to you in order to overcome.

This help can come from your "Inner Circle." John C. Maxwell teaches in his books on the value of having an Inner Circle. It is important as a leader to have a close group that you can confide in and trust to help you thru difficult times. Without that Inner Circle a leader can lose hope and lose commitment. Once commitment and hope are lost, all is lost for the leader. He or she will fall to the bottom and have to attempt to one day regain the momentum, trust, and commitment they once had.

Keep your perspective in order to overcome adversity. Never lose sight of what the ultimate goal is and what you are trying to accomplish. Abraham Lincoln ran for multiple political offices before he ever won an election. He faced adversity many times, but he never lost perspective and ultimately became The President of The United States of America. Just because you are tested with adversity does not mean that you will not reach your goal. It just means that it's going to take longer than you first expected, but as long as you are committed you will overcome.

Pat Riley once said, "There are only two options regarding commitment. You're either in or out. There's no such thing as a life in-between." Remembering that you have to be committed is a key to facing adversity. If you are not committed, you will fail in the face of adversity. There are no exceptions to that just as Mr. Riley said with being "in or out." You cannot straddle the fence of commitment. You are either committed or you're not. Do not attempt to try to be in between or you will lose all you have gained.

Zig Ziglar was quoted as saying, "Sometimes adversity is what you need to face in order to become successful." He is entirely correct with that statement. You will not be successful if you do not face adversity because your commitment will never be tested. To be a truly successful leader, you have to be tested - just as Job was tested to see if he was truly a God fearing man. Commitment has to be tested whether we like it or not. It is part of the leadership journey. Being able to face adversity and pass the commitment test will lead you to becoming a better leader. If you look back thru history at all the great leaders, they all faced adversity in order to test their commitment. There is not a single one that got to skip that step. Not even the Son of God, Jesus Christ, was able to skip facing adversity. We all have to face adversity in order to show our commitment.

In his book *Home Run,* Kevin Myers sums up Job's adversity and commitment by saying:

> "This desire to understand God and His workings is as old as humankind. It was present in the Garden of Eden. And it's evident in the book of Job, one of the oldest writings in the Bible. Job believed he was living a righteous life, yet he suffered horrible calamity: the death of his children, the loss of his possessions, and untold pain and physical suffering. His wife told him to curse God and die. His friends admonished him to confess his hidden sin. Job revered God, but he wanted to know what God was up to. Job felt he couldn't go on, yet he wouldn't quit on God. Only when Job recognized his own powerlessness was he able to accept his life. And in the end, God had new dreams for Job (3)."

JOSEPH

Joseph used dreams to prepare the Visions he needed to help the Egyptians.

Joseph was destined to be a great leader from the beginning. As a youth, Joseph knew God had something great in store for him. At an early age, Joseph had a dream from God that he used as a vision for his future. In Genesis 37: 5, 6, and 9-11 (NKJV), it states:

> "Now Joseph had a dream, and he told it to his brothers; and they hated him even more. So he said to them, "Please hear this dream which I have dreamed:" Then he dreamed still another dream and told it to his brothers, and said, "Look, I have dreamed another dream. And this time, the sun, the moon, and the eleven stars bowed down to me." So he told it to his father and his brothers; and is father rebuked him and said to him, "What is this dream that you have dreamed? Shall

your mother and I and your brothers indeed come to bow down to the earth before you?" And his brothers envied him, but his father kept the matter in mind."

Joseph was given a dream by God in order to show him his future. However, no one else was on-board with the dream when Joseph shared it. In fact, his family hated him for his dreams. God was using this as the beginning of great things for Joseph. Joseph was going to endure some hardships along the way, but in the end great things were going to happen to him. Joseph was going to be able to cast visions for his followers in order to be a great leader.

Let's start looking more in depth into Joseph's leadership qualities by first defining dreams and visions. A dream is defined as "a series of thoughts, visions, or feelings that happen during sleep or an idea or vision that is created in your imagination and that is not real (4)." Now, a vision is defined as "the ability to see or something that you imagine – a picture that you see in your mind (5)." As you can see in the definitions dreams and visions go hand in hand. They are both things that you imagine in your mind. As a leader it's what you do with them that matters. Being able to share the dream and vision with your followers is what leads to becoming a great leader.

There are a few qualities that help a leader share his or her dreams and visions with their followers. Those qualities that I want to share are patience, humility, and wisdom. First, let us look at patience.

Patience

Patience is the habit of being patient. We all know that patience is hard to come by and hard to grasp. We all have things or people that know how to push our buttons and make us lose patience. Have you ever prayed for patience? If you have, you know how tough it is to gain. It seems like when we pray for patience then God sends things our way that will test our patience. God uses this to teach us patience instead of giving it to us automatically. Patience is something that is acquired not something that is given.

If we look back through the scripture, we can see that Joseph exhibited a lot of patience. The first example of this was in regards to his brothers. His brothers continued to hate him as time went by because of his dreams and the fact that he was their father's favorite. However, Joseph did not let this deter him from greatness. He continued living his life in order to fulfill his potential. Second, Joseph was sold into slavery by his brothers. Instead of fighting this, he went to Egypt and began using his leadership to find favor in the sight of his masters. He patiently awaited his time to do great things. Third, he interpreted two dreams for the Pharaoh's chief butler and chief baker and asked them to remember him to their master; however, once they were called back to Pharaoh they did not remember him. Joseph had to remain in prison awhile longer. Finally, Joseph's time arrived when Pharaoh needed someone to interpret a dream and he was told about Joseph. Joseph's patience paid off and now his time to lead people and cast visions had arrived.

Humility

The next quality that Joseph used was humility. This was a good quality for Joseph to have because humility is hard to come by. Joseph used humility to not throw his gifts in his brothers' faces. He was humble with his gifts and used them when needed. William Temple said, "Humility does not mean thinking less of yourself than of other people, nor does it mean having a low opinion of your own gifts. It means freedom from thinking about yourself at all." Being a good leader means you are humble. You do not boast or pat yourself on the back. You are genuine on being yourself and understanding your gifts but not shoving them in the face of others.

Wisdom

Finally, Joseph had wisdom. Wisdom is knowledge that is gained by having many experiences in life. Wisdom is a quality that you learn and gain throughout life. It is not something that you have automatically. Joseph was able to gain wisdom thru the good and bad experiences that he had in life. He was able to use those experiences to help cast his visions to help Egypt in their upcoming crisis.

Thomas Jefferson once said, "Honesty is the first chapter in the book of wisdom." This is completely true. In order to gain wisdom, you must first be honest with yourself and with others.

You will not gain wisdom if you are not honest because you will always hide from the truth of the experiences you go thru in life.

Finally, Doug Larson said, "Wisdom is the reward you get for a lifetime of listening when you'd have preferred to talk." You gain wisdom not only from listening to others but from listening to lessons that life is trying to teach you from the experiences and the adversity that it throws at you. You also gain wisdom from listening to God. God tries to teach all of us experiences by talking to us. In order for us to gain wisdom from Him, we have to listen to Him.

Now, that we have looked at three qualities that Joseph possessed in order to cast visions, we can now look at what visions can do for a leader, their followers, and their organizations. Joseph used his dreams and interpretations of dreams to cast the visions he needed to help lead the Egyptians. Visions are key to reaching your goals as a leader. You have to cast the vision and get buy-in in order to make it happen. Remember that casting the vision takes patience, wisdom, and humility.

Jonathan Swift said, "Vision is the art of seeing what is invisible to others." As a leader you share a vision with your people that at first they will not see. You will then have to share the vision with them many times in order to get buy-in and eventually succeed in achieving the vision. You will have to paint the picture to them in order for them to see it. Vision casting is a quality that is hard for some leaders to achieve, but to be successful you must share visions with your people.

The main dream that Joseph interpreted and used as a vision to the people is found in Genesis 41. Joseph shared the interpretation of the dream starting at verse 25 and it states:

> "Then Joseph said to Pharaoh, "The dreams of Pharaoh are one; God has shown Pharaoh what He is about to do: The seven good cows are seven years, and the seven good heads are seven years; the dreams are one. And the seven thin and ugly cows which came up after them are seven years, and the seven empty heads blighted by the east wind are seven years of famine (NKJV)."

God then used Joseph to help lead Egypt into and out of the famine that was coming. Joseph shared his vision with the people and they listened as they prepared for the famine. Another bonus from this is that Joseph was reunited with his brothers and father due to the famine and his original dream was a reality. Joseph led the people to success during the bad times, a tribute to the success of his leadership abilities.

Sharing the vision is the first step to reach success. The second step is having action behind that vision. Visions do not achieve success on their own; they have to have action behind them. Joel A. Barker said, "Vision without action is merely a dream. Action without vision just passes time. Vision with action can change the world." As a leader, you have to put action behind the vision that you cast with your people. You cannot stand by and expect them to achieve results without your help. You have to take action as well. Working together and acting together leads to the success of the vision.

Organizations in today's world have visions and mission statements about the way they want to accomplish their success. They cast visions to lead their workers to the success they want to achieve. Let's look at a few:

- Academy Sports + Outdoors vision is to be the premier sports, outdoor, and lifestyle store of choice, continuously adapting to our customers' changing needs (6).
- General Electric wants to be a company that is always getting better (7).
- Target wants to be your preferred shopping destination in all channels by fulfilling their Expect More/Pay Less promise (8).

Visions are not only important to individuals but to organizations as well. Do not be afraid to share your vision. You need all your people to be on-board in order for the vision to be successful. Take action and lead your team to success just as Joseph did with the Egyptians. Joseph reached his potential and made the difference thanks to visions.

MOSES

God chose Moses to communicate to and for the Children of Israel.

The next leader that we will look at thru our journey of biblical leaders is Moses. Moses was chosen by God to be the key communicator for the Children of Israel. God used Moses to communicate key items to the Children of Israel and for the Children of Israel. As a leader, being able to communicate is a key quality. If you cannot communicate, you will never be able to be an effective leader because you will not be able to tell your people the vision or the goals you have for them. You will also not be able to communicate key things to them. Communication is extremely valuable to a leader. Through this section of the book, we will look at Moses and examine how he communicated and learn ways to be an effective communicator.

If your first thought after reading that communication is a key is that I am not good at communicating, then you are not alone. Moses was afraid to be a communicator at first. We see in Exodus 3:11 thru 4:14 that Moses attempted to use excuses to keep from being chosen by God to communicate. Moses used five excuses in attempt to tell God that he was not the right person. Those excuses were:

1. Who am I?
2. Who are you?
3. What if they do not listen?
4. I've never been a good speaker.
5. I know you can find someone else (9).

The good news is that even though Moses tried to make excuses God would not accept them. He was chosen and God was going to use him. Do not be afraid if you are not a great communicator. You can learn to develop skills in order to be a better communicator. As a leader, you cannot shy away from communication even if you are uncomfortable with it. You have to work on it to become better.

Now that we see that it is okay to be afraid to communicate, let's look at why Moses ended up being a great communicator.

God Spoke Thru Him

The first key to Moses success as a communicator is that God spoke thru him. This meant that God helped him become a great communicator. God gave Moses the tools he needed to communicate to Pharaoh and to the Children of Israel. If you look back thru all the great preachers in our lifetime, I can guarantee you that they were all not great communicators at first. God helped them become great communicators over time. Very few people are great communicators at first. Most people and most leaders develop this quality over time.

Consistent

The second key is that Moses was consistent when speaking to Pharaoh. In order to communicate a message, you have to be consistent. Every time Moses went to Pharaoh, he delivered the same message. He asked Pharaoh to let the Children of Israel go in order for them to go and bring sacrifices to God. Once Pharaoh said no, then Moses told him about the plague that was to be brought upon them. He was consistent to deliver the same message to Pharaoh every time. He was not "wishy washy." As a leader, we have to communicate the same message every time in order for us to reach our followers. We cannot share one message with one person and a different message with another person. We have to communicate the same message in order to keep everyone on the same page and in order to reach the same goals.

Credible

The next key we look at is that Moses was credible. The Children of Israel listened to Moses because they learned to trust him and the message he was communicating. Every time Moses communicated something to his followers, it came true. His followers learned to trust him due to this. Thus it became easier for him to communicate with his followers because he was trusted by them. As a leader, you can get a lot accomplished when your people trust you.

Clear Communication

Another key is clear communication. When communicating with people, your communication must be clear and to the point.

You cannot paint a fuzzy picture to your people or your message will never be received. Ben Jonson said, "To speak and to speak well are two things. A fool may talk, but a wise man speaks." In order to have clear communication, you have to speak well. Speaking well means you are painting the clear picture your people need.

John C. Maxwell, from his Leadership Bible, says this about clear communication – "Without the ability to communicate, a leader travels alone. No one will catch your vision unless you first transfer a picture of it into his or her heart. That's what God did when he clearly explained to the Hebrew families how they could spare the lives of their first born sons (10)."

Finally, without clear communication, a follower would be like a person trying to put a puzzle together without the picture. Think about it. Have you ever tried to put a puzzle together without the picture on the box? If you haven't, try it. You will quickly see that it is extremely difficult. The picture of the puzzle paints the clear picture needed to successfully complete the puzzle. It's the same with clear communication. Clear communication paints the clear picture needed for your followers to succeed.

Calm

Next, we see that Moses remained calm when communicating. The first example of this is when Moses went to talk to Pharaoh. Each time Moses spoke to Pharaoh he was calm and never lost his cool even though it probably angered him that he had to go to Pharaoh multiple times to get his point across. Another example of this is the many times that he communicated to the Children of Israel. They tried him many times but he remained calm. He never lost patience in front of them.

As a leader, there will be trying times or trying people that will attempt to make you angry. You must remain calm in these situations. It will mean more to your people to see you stay calm in times of adversity than for you to lose it. You do not need to lose patience or act crazy to get you point across. If you remain calm, your point will be delivered more promptly than you think it will.

Moses remained calm thru most situations with the Children of Israel; however, he did have a moment of weakness and was not able to remain calm. We see this in Numbers 20:7-12 when he smote the rock twice to get water for the Children of Israel. Due to this error in judgment, Moses was not allowed to take his people into the Promised Land. If we do not remain calm as leaders, then we will suffer the consequences that we otherwise would be able to avoid.

Confidence

Another key is to be confident. When communicating with your people, you must be confident. Your people are looking for your confidence. If you try to deliver a message and you are not confident, your message will not be received. People do not follow leaders that lack confidence. They also do not listen to leaders that do not speak or communicate with confidence. Your people want to see and hear confidence when you are communicating with them. But be careful in this area as you do not want to come off cocky or arrogant. There is a fine line between confidence and arrogance. As a leader, you do not need to cross that line. You will lose your people if you are arrogant.

Competent

Next, you need to be competent. When you are communicating, you have to be competent. This means knowing what you are communicating. You cannot communicate your message if you are not competent in what you are trying to portray to your people. Take time to research and rehearse your message before you communicate it. The worst thing you can do is go unprepared to communicate a message. Your people will not listen because they will think that you have no clue about what you are talking about.

Simplicity

The final key is simplicity. Keep the message being communicated simple. Colin Powell said, "Great leaders are almost always great simplifiers." Keep things simple. If you keep the message simple, your people will grasp it easier and be able to succeed quicker. Simplicity is a leader's best friend. Remember the KISS rule – "Keep It Simple, Stupid." The simpler something is the easier it is for people to respond to it. Do not make communication become a physics problem.

As a leader, communication is the key to our success. Without it, you will not succeed. You have to be committed to it. Moses committed himself to communication even though he struggled with it. You can also commit yourself to communication. Work on the keys above and you will become a better communicator. Never underestimate the power of communication. If you do, you will fail as a leader because no one will be able to hear your message.

The final point on communication comes from John C. Maxwell's *The 21 Irrefutable Laws of Leadership.* That point is "The Law of Navigation." John writes that "Anyone can steer the ship, but it takes a leader to chart the course (11)." As a leader, communication charts the course that you need to navigate the vision you have for your people. Without communication, your people are going to navigate around and around but never reach their destination. As a leader, helping our followers reach their destination is a top priority. They are relying on us to help them get there. Communicate to them and help them reach their destination.

JOSHUA

Joshua builds momentum as a leader.

In John Maxwell's *The 21 Irrefutable Laws of Leadership,* he talks about the "Law of the Big Mo." In the "Law of the Big Mo," John says that "momentum is a leader's best friend (12)." That statement is completely true. Momentum means everything to a leader. Without it nothing will be accomplished and success will be out of reach. Momentum is a key in a lot of areas in life. Just look at sports. There are a lot of examples we can look at in the sports world to see that momentum is a key factor. It is no different in leadership. A leader with momentum will go on and continue to succeed and do great things. A leader without momentum will stay dormant.

In this chapter, we will take a look at two types of people that affect momentum, how decisions affect momentum, and ways to help build or gain momentum. Before we look at each of those areas, we need to talk about one key to momentum. That key is timing. Momentum is all about timing. Timing means everything when it comes to momentum. When you look at Joshua Chapter 1, you quickly see how timing affects momentum. God knew what type of leader he needed to take the Children of Israel to the next step. It was time to go to the Promised Land and in order to do so they needed a military style leader and in comes Joshua. Joshua was able to use momentum to do what he needed to do in order to follow God's Plan. Now let's look at how Joshua used momentum.

Results Matter

When it comes to building momentum, results matter. You cannot build momentum without gaining positive results. If the results are negative, then the people on your team will begin to become negative and gain the attitude that they will never achieve the goal ahead of them.

The following diagram shows how results matter when it

comes to momentum as well as ties in timing. There are two times to make a decision as a leader - the right time and the wrong time. Each one effects momentum differently. When a leader makes a decision at the right time, he or she builds momentum. When a leader makes a decision at the wrong time, he or she kills

momentum.

Right Time

Wrong Time

In order to build momentum, a leader must make decisions at the right time. You may be thinking how do I know the right time? As a leader, you learn when decisions need to be made. There is not a book out there that can tell you when timing is correct to make the decision. You learn this from experience. There will be many times as a leader that you will make a decision at the wrong time. The key is to learn from it and move forward in your leadership.

Wins

"Wins" help gain momentum. Everyone likes to see positive results and to see the team "win." This was a key to Joshua's success as a leader. As you read thru the first chapters of the book of Joshua, you see that Joshua led the Children of Israel to quick wins against cities and armies in the Promised Land. These quick "wins" helped the Children of Israel build momentum heading into the bigger battles that were ahead of them.

Henry Ford once said, "Coming together is a beginning, keeping together is progress, working together is success." In order to achieve "wins," a leader must bring his team together and help them work together. When the team works together and succeeds, the "wins" come and the momentum builds. Make sure, as a leader, that you help your team get a few "wins" under their belt before you go after the big goals. Get them the confidence and the momentum they need to continue the progress toward the goal.

Navigate

As a leader, you have to navigate your people to gain momentum. Your team will not always know where to start in order to achieve the desired results. You, at times, will have to show them the way. To paint a better picture, you will sometimes have to give them the roadmap to get where they are going. There will be times when your team will not be able to see the big picture, which is when you will have to navigate for them to see it.

You can read throughout the book of Joshua and see where Joshua had to navigate the Children of Israel back on course. The Children of Israel had the problem of forgetting who brought them to where they were. They would forget God and do their own thing. Joshua had to intercede for them and navigate them back on course in order to keep their momentum in the Promised Land.

Zig Ziglar said, "People often say that motivation doesn't last. Well, neither does bathing – that's why we recommend it daily." In order to navigate your team, you will have to motivate them. Just remember that you will have to do this daily. Motivation is a daily process, not a weekly or monthly process. Motivation ties to navigation because you have to sometimes motivate your people to stay on track.

Integrity

To build momentum or to continue momentum, you must have integrity. Integrity is a big key to a leader. For this section, we will look at why integrity is important to momentum. It will not take long to see why. We can look at many examples to see why it is important.

The first example that comes to mind to me is Enron. This company was on a huge momentum swing and growing to new heights, until its leaders started doing things that lacked integrity. Once that happened, the company went downhill. Enron went under, the executives went to prison, and employees lost their livelihood.

As a leader you can lack integrity in your decisions and get away with it momentarily, but it will not last long. Integrity will always catch up with you and win in the end. Stay on the right side of that line and your momentum will continue. Cross to the other side, and you will watch your success implode and hurt the ones around you.

Confidence

The last thing we will look at when it comes to momentum is confidence. When momentum builds, so does confidence. There is nothing wrong with gaining confidence as a team. It's how you use it that can become the problem.

In the book of Genesis, we see a prime example of confidence and momentum being used in the wrong way. This starts in Genesis 11:4, when the people of Babel wanted to build a tower to heaven. The people got overconfident and made a plan that would seal doom for them. Because of their arrogance, God changed the languages of the people which created confusion and lead to their momentum being halted.

Use momentum and confidence together for the good of the people and the team, not for the good of the individual. Leadership is about influencing others to achieve goals not about you gaining notoriety and prosperity.

The last thing, I want to share with you in regards to momentum is the two types of people when it comes to momentum. In life, we have momentum breakers and momentum makers. Hopefully, on your team, you will have more momentum makers than breakers. Your team will build momentum faster with makers. You can build momentum with breakers on your team, but it will be very challenging.

It will cause headaches and stress to your team and you will have to find ways to keep the team together. If your team has breakers on it, my suggestion would be to find ways to get them onboard. If you cannot, then you need to remove them from your team. Do not let breakers stay around too long because if you do your makers will leave and then you will lose all momentum.

Joshua did a good job of keeping the momentum on the side of the Children of Israel during his reign as their leader. It was not all smooth sailing, but he made it thru. He made momentum last with probably the hardest team in history to do so. That's what makes him the prime example as a leader that built momentum. Your team will never be as hard to lead as the Children of Israel, but you will still face challenges when it comes to momentum. Remember to navigate them thru and build those "wins" and your team will build the momentum it needs.

RUTH

Ruth shows how listening can lead to great things.

As a leader, we are constantly communicating to our followers. It feels like we do most of the talking throughout a project or a meeting. We sometimes forget that we have another important area that we must excel at that does not involve us speaking. That area is listening. There are times when our followers need us to lend an ear and listen to them. Listening does not always come easy for leaders. It is something we must all work at because we do not want our followers to feel like we do not care about them. Not listening to our followers can cause them to hold things in and be disruptive to the team because they feel their needs are not being met.

A prime example of a leader in the Bible that listened was Ruth. When we read the book of Ruth, we see how she used her listening skills lead to great things for herself and her family. The first thing she did was to willingly follow Naomi – which we read about in Ruth 1:8-18. She left her comfort zone and followed Naomi back to Bethlehem. Ruth left everything she had ever known to make this journey with her mother-in-law. Once they arrived in Bethlehem, Ruth then submitted herself to the directions that Naomi gave her day-in and day-out. She listened to Naomi and followed her directions and advice in order to succeed. Due to her listening to Naomi, Ruth was able to do many great things as well as met her husband Boaz in Bethlehem.

It was once said that great leaders know how to be great followers. If that is the case, then when we as leaders were followers we had times that we needed our leader to listen to us. We had needs and concerns that needed to be addressed and needed someone to listen to us. We all have had times in our lives that we needed someone to lend us an ear and to hear our issues. Think about those people in your life that you always counted on to listen to you. What characteristics did they have when it came to being a good listener?

Now that you have had a minute to think and decide those key characteristics, let's take a look into the key characteristics that I believe leaders should have to be good listeners.

Commitment

As a leader, I feel the first characteristic you need to be a listener is commitment. You have to be committed to listening to others. If you are not committed to listening to what your followers need or what they are concerned about, then they will feel that you are only looking out for yourself. You never want to give off the impression that you do not care about your people. This will only make things more difficult on you down the road.

J. Isham once said, "Listening is an attitude of the heart, a genuine desire to be with another which both attracts and heals." To be committed to listening, you have to have that attitude in your heart. That attitude is the attitude of caring. We will discuss caring next in this chapter. Be committed to your people and listen to them. It will only make your team stronger.

Caring

The next thing that listening requires is caring. You have to have a genuine caring attitude and heart. A true leader cares about his people and wants to be there for them when they need it. A true leader never pushes his or her people away. They are there for the long haul and want to be there anytime they are needed. Showing your people that you care will lead them to trust you and respect you because they know they can count on you.

Followers want to work for a leader that cares and the main way you can show them you care is by listening. They want you to listen to them because they have concerns, thoughts, issues, etc. that need to be addressed. Let's look at a list of things they want you to listen to:

1. They have ideas for the team
2. They have a concern about a team member
3. They feel overlooked
4. They have an issue at home
5. They are concerned about you
6. They do not feel valued

Those are a few of the many things that your team members may want to discuss with you and want you to hear their thoughts and concerns. They want you to care about these issues and listen to them and finally help them where you can. They do not want you to sweep them "under the rug." Paul Dietzal said, "There are no office hours for champions." As a leader, to show that you care and that you are there for your team, you have to be available at all times. Being a leader is not a 9 to 5 job. It is a 24/7 job. Great leaders know that and they are not afraid to be there for their team when needed no matter the time.

Active Listening

Being a good listener requires you to be an active listener. You may be asking, what is an active listener? An active listener is a person that listens but also responds back when the time is right. They also repeat back to show the person that they understand. They ask questions to make sure they are on the same page. An active listener knows when to talk and when to listen in the conversation.

Lyndon B. Johnson said it best when he said, "There are no

problems we cannot solve together and very few that we can solve by ourselves." Active listeners are there to help. They are there to help with the problems and to offer solutions when needed. Two people solving the problem are better than one. Johnson also said, "You aren't learning anything when you're talking." As an active listener, you have to listen so you can hear what the person is saying. In order to know how and when to respond you have to listen to them.

Requires Response

Next, listening requires a response. Most people want to hear the leader's response once they are finished sharing. There are occasions in which a response may not be required. If you are in that situation, you will be able to tell if you need to respond or not. Followers want you to respond because they will then know you are listening to them and that you care about their concerns.

The second part to requiring a response is that you have to be credible when responding. Your people need to know that they can trust your response. Give them honest answers and honest feedback. Do not give them the answer you feel they want to hear.

Give them the honest truth. Your team will respect you more in the long run if you do so.

Requires Risk

Listening also requires risk. Leaders take risk when they are listeners because they know they need to be honest to their people. Honesty is not always taken well by the person it is given to at first. Risk is also taken because the issue being discussed could involve the leader. It could be constructive criticism that we need to hear. Finally, risk is taken because you may not know where the conversation will head and you fear you will not know how to respond. The good news is that as leaders we are equipped with four traits that allow us to take the risk when it comes to listening. They are:

1. Responsibility
2. Initiative
3. Sacrifice
4. Knowledge

With those four traits, we can respond to the issues we are listening to and be able to take the risk needed to be the listener our people need us to be.

To wrap-up this chapter on listening and how it is important to a leader, I want to share a statement from John C. Maxwell. This came from his book *Leadership Gold.* John wrote in his book the following:

Why listeners make effective leaders...
1. Listening is the best way to learn
2. Listening can keep problems from escalating
3. Listening can improve the organization (13)

All three of these are key ways that make listeners effective leaders. If you are able to listen to your people, then you will be able to lead your people. A Cherokee Proverb says, "Listen to the whispers and you won't have to hear the screams." Listen to your people and you will be able to lead a successful team. That's why listening is important!

GIDEON

Gideon exemplifies how a leader needs influence on his side.

John C. Maxwell defines leadership as follows, "All leadership is influence." That is the essential key of leadership. As a leader you must influence people to be successful. Without influence, there is no leadership. Webster's Dictionary defines leadership as "the power to change or affect someone or something (14)." So as a leader, we must be able to change or affect the people that we come in contact with and the people that we lead. One of the best examples of this in the Bible is Gideon. We can see Gideon's story in Judges 6:11 thru 8:35.

Dwight D. Eisenhower said, "Leadership is the art of getting someone else to do something you want done because he wants to do it." This definition of leadership ties right back to the fact that leadership is influence. As a leader, your influence should have your people doing things because they want to not because you told them to. If they are doing things because you told them to, then you are not influencing them. You are simply using authority against them. Ken Blanchard was quoted saying, "The key to successful leadership today is influence not authority."

As we look into Gideon's story in this chapter, the first thing I want to talk about is the "Seven Assets Followers Want in a Leader (15)." These assets help create influence among your followers. The assets are as follows:

1. Calling
2. Insight
3. Charisma
4. Talent
5. Ability
6. Communication
7. Character

These are the seven key areas that every leader must have to be successful. We will look at each of these in depth to better understand why they are assets that followers want in you as a leader.

Calling

First is calling. Every leader has to have a calling to lead. There is a question out there that many people ask about leaders. That question is "Are leaders born or made?" The answer is that leaders are made and this is seen when it comes to having a calling to be a leader. You can develop yourself into a leader by studying and learning all you can about it. You do not have to be born a leader. Everyone does not have the calling to be a leader. It takes someone with dedication and ability to be a leader. Gideon was an unlikely leader that God called into leadership. Gideon was so surprised that he questioned his calling at first. He actually questioned it twice before he accepted God's will.

You do not have to be born with the insights of a leader. If you have the calling, you can develop yourself to be a leader. There are many ways to develop yourself to be a leader. You can read, attend workshops, and watch videos to name a few. There are so many resources out there for you to use to your advantage. Just because you think you lack the qualities needed to be a leader does not mean that you neglect the calling. If you have the calling to be a leader that means that God has something great in store for your life and your leadership. You just have to take the initiative to develop yourself to reach that potential.

Insight

Second, we look at insight. Insight is the ability to be able to see what others cannot see. A leader needs insight in order to find answers and solutions. A leader has to be able to make decisions using his or her insights when there seems to be no solution. There are times that the team needs insight in order to move forward. That is when a leader must step in.

Everyone does not have the gift of insight. You have to learn to have it. Having insight comes from trial and error. It comes from making decisions that are not always correct. It comes from failure and from learning from that failure. You gain insight thru your experiences. Followers want leaders who can share insight and help them thru situations that arise. If you do not have insight and cannot share it, you will not lead your team to success and you will not be able to influence your team.

Gideon gained insight that he shared with his team when he went down to the Midianites camp before they attacked. God gave Gideon the insight needed to be successful that night and to ensure that the men would not be scared to go to battle. Insight helps all teams become successful because it helps them know where they are going.

Charisma

Third, a leader needs charisma. A leader needs to be excited and needs to challenge their people. A leader has to have energy and carry that where ever they go. Without energy people will not follow you. They feed off of your energy and that helps them continue to succeed with the vision or goal at hand.

Have you ever had a leader that lacked charisma? If so, you know you do not do your best for them. On the other hand, think about the leader you had that was charismatic. I bet you would run thru a wall for them. Charisma is an asset that helps you push your team. It helps you motivate them when they are down, it helps spark that energy when they are tired, and it helps push them when they can barely see the finish line. Charisma is a momentum changer and can turn you toward success when there does not seem to be a way.

Talent

Fourth, a leader has to have talent. A leader has to have the talent to exemplify and show leadership. Not everyone has the talent to do this. The good news is that you can teach yourself the talent of leadership just like you can teach yourself the talent of singing or playing music. There are many tools out there to help you learn leadership and learn the skills and abilities you need to be a leader and establish the talent needed.

Everyone has a talent, you just have to find what talent is yours. What gift did God give to you to benefit the world? Some have the talent of music, some the talent of speech, some the talent of writing, some the talent of prayer. The list can go on and on. Leadership is a talent. Either you have it or you do not. There will be people on your team that you want to develop into a leader, but they will not have the talent needed to do so. Not everyone has what it takes to be a leader. Do not push people without the talent to be a leader. You will only frustrate yourself, them, and your team.

Ability

Fifth, a leader needs ability. A leader has to have ability in order to lead. This is where influence comes back into play. A leader has to have the ability to influence people. Gideon had influence because he was called by God to be a leader. Without influence, Gideon would not have been able to have 32,000 men join him to fight the Midianites at first. Gideon's influence and ability gave him an army that was great in size to go in battle for Israel.

Communication

Sixth, a leader has to have communication. Communication is extremely important in leadership. Without communication, everyone would be lost. No one would know what to do and what to accomplish. There would be no goal, vision, or plan because no one would have communicated it. If you cannot communicate, you cannot lead. People have to know the game plan and have to know how to get there to accomplish it. This asset is so important that we have devoted an entire chapter to it earlier in the book.

Character

Finally, a leader has to have character. Character helps build and maintain trust with your people. Your team has to know that they can count on you to do the right thing. They have to know that you are honest, trustworthy, and loyal to them. There has to be integrity in all you do and how you do it. Most leaders fail because they lack integrity. If your team cannot trust you, they will not succeed for you. If you ever lose trust with your team, you might as well walk away because you will not gain it back. People normally only give you one chance. Do not destroy that chance because of character flaws. Do the right thing all the time – even if it's the unpopular decision. In the end, you will be glad you did.

Once a leader knows and can show that they have the seven assets, then they can move forward with influence. John C. Maxwell wrote about the "Law of Influence" in his book *The 21 Irrefutable Law of Leadership*. It says, "The true measure of leadership is influence – nothing more, nothing less (16)."

Influence is key with everything leadership. Without influence, Gideon would not have been successful in leading the Israelites against the Midianites.

Influence helped Gideon achieve another one of John C. Maxwell's leadership laws as well. That is the "Law of Buy-In," which says "People buy-in to the leader, then the vision (17)." With 32,000 men showing up to battle with Gideon, we can see that the people bought into him as a leader. We also see that after God wanted less people to battle that this buy-in was even stronger because the final number of men went from 32,000 to 300. Those 300 men must have really bought into Gideon as their leader in order to go to battle against a bigger army. If your team has bought into you, there is nothing that you can't accomplish. Remember not to destroy buy-in by destroying trust or establishing an ego. We will take a more detailed look at how ego can destroy a leader in our next chapter as we look into the life of Samson.

The biggest challenge that a leader will face when it comes to influence will be authority. We spoke quickly about it in the first part of this chapter, but I want to spend a little more time on it now

to help you understand the pitfalls of authority. Leaders that have
to use authority to get things done are not good leaders and will not
be in a leadership position long. People will not follow a leader
that is authoritative. Those types of leaders lack character and
charisma as well as the other assets of leadership. These leaders
rely on their position to get things done and to have people follow
them. It will only work for them for a short period of time.

A leader cannot rely on a position or a title to get things done.
It takes more than that to be a leader and to influence people.
Think back on past leaders you have worked for. I bet you can
think of a few that used authority to lead. I also bet you did not like
following them and you were not there long before you moved to
another leader. People leave leaders not organizations. This can be
seen when it comes to leaders lacking influence. People want to be
influenced and they want to learn from a leader that they buy into.
People do not buy into leaders that are positional. Leadership is a
"what have you done for me lately" business not a "what have I
done for the leader" business.

Influence your people and help develop them for the next

level. Do not hold them back or they will leave you for another leader who will propel them forward. Booker T. Washington said it best when he said, "There is not power on earth that can neutralize the influence of a high, simple and useful life." As leaders, we should all strive to influence all that we can. Remember that all leadership is influence. Influence people and you will have mastered leadership. Leadership is simple. We just make it more complicated than we need to do so. If you take one thing from this book, I want it to be this:

"Leadership is Influence – Nothing More, Nothing Less"

- John C. Maxwell

SAMSON

Samson shows how a leader's ego can harm his leadership and his team.

Most of this book is about positive leadership characteristics; however, I wanted to put a chapter in the book that points out a negative leadership characteristic. This is a characteristic that leaders struggle with that can cause problems if it is not controlled. The characteristic is ego. Everyone has an ego not just leaders. Some people do a better job of controlling it than others. Ego is not easy to control. We all like to be congratulated and to have the feeling of accomplishment. We like positive gratification about our accomplishments. Those things boost our egos. As leaders, we have to control that ego. It is even harder to do as a leader. There are many leaders in the Bible that struggled with ego, but for this case I have picked the one I feel most exemplifies the quality.

The prime example that we will look at when it comes to ego is Samson. He was the strongest man alive and was called by God to do great things. We can read his entire story in Judges Chapters 13 thru 16. Samson was primed to do great things until his ego got in the way. Samson gave into the sins of the flesh and it cost him greatly. Samson met Delilah which ultimately changed his course. He let her build his ego by attacking his weaknesses and he ultimately told her the secret to his strength. She then used that information against Samson and he lost all he built as a leader.

We can look back thru history and see many leaders who have allowed their ego to derail their success and their influence. Their decisions then cost their teams, their families, and ultimately themselves. The really bad news to this is that it actually cost people that they did not even know. This can be seen with examples of the leaders of Enron. Their egos ultimately cost stockholders and employees that they did not have relationships with. Ego harms more people than you actually realize. That is why we as leaders have to work hard to control it and keep it in check. Always understand that you will have an ego – you cannot get rid of it. You just have to learn to keep it in check and understand the actions that can happen if you do not.

You may be wondering why it is so important to talk about ego and why spend an entire chapter dedicated to it. It is important because too many people including leaders fall victim to it. In order to prevent others from falling victim, I feel it is important to discuss it and ensure that all who read this understands it. I'm going to make a big statement here that I hope you agree with. Egos can get in a leader's way and cause them to fail. When I say this not only do I mean the leader's ego but also the egos of all the people on the team. A leader has to learn how to control all egos around them. If they see a problem arising they have to address it and keep it in check. I understand that all this is easier said than done, but the reality is most leaders do not know how to recognize these problems because they cannot control their own egos.

We live in a society that rewards taking big risk. We reward CEOs with six to seven figure annual compensation, bonuses, private jets, and expense accounts. We reward athletes with seven to eight figure compensation. We award people millions for suing someone or some business for anything no matter whose fault it is. We have developed a society that strokes egos. The more you take a risk, the more you get rewarded. The more you get rewarded, the more your ego grows. We do not have a system in place to keep egos in check. If we do not address this then the next generation of leaders are going to assume they have to have a big ego to succeed. This really hurts me as a leader because the opposite is true. You do not have to have an ego to succeed. All the ego does is increase your chances at huge failures as a leader. You may get by for a while with your ego, but mark my words – it will catch up with you and you will fall and fail. And when you do, there will be no one there to pick you up. You will have hit "Leadership Rock Bottom."

When we talk about ego, we must first understand that there is a fine line between confidence and cockiness. As a leader, you have to walk the line and walk it well. This is where the first issues arise. Being cocky feeds your ego. In order to control our ego and keep it in check, we must not feed our egos. We have to remain humble and not become prideful. The best leaders do not accept the credit, the pass it down to their team. That's because they understand that the team is the reason why they are where they are. They understand that it's not about "me" but rather about "we." You must learn to pass the praise to those who deserve it and not keep it to yourself. If you keep it to yourself then you will start enlarging your ego.

Ego is all psychological. It is mental and only you can control it. No one else can help you control something that is mental. If you keep success to yourself, then it will build in your psyche. The more it builds the worse it gets. This leads to the next point. After a leader tastes success, then they feel that they have arrived and ultimately lose touch with reality. The best leaders understand that they never arrive. There is always something to learn, someone to develop, and something to achieve. You never truly arrive. In my opinion, a leader never arrives until he or she passes on. That is when they leave their legacy and reach the ultimate "Pinnacle Level of Leadership (18)" that John C. Maxwell writes about in his book *The Five Levels of Leadership.* While a leader is still leading, they are still arriving. Leadership is about learning and developing and there is always something to learn and someone to develop into a future leader.

In the next part of this chapter, I want to address a few areas that need to be looked at to keep your ego in check:

Pride

Pride is a big area to watch when it comes to ego. Pride causes you to be become proud of your accomplishment and to soak in the accolades of the success. Pride has caused a lot of people to fall throughout history. When I say history, I'm including the biblical times as well. You do not have to look very far for an example of pride causing issues for mankind. We can see God talk about pride in the Bible multiple times:

> Proverbs 11:2, "When pride comes, then comes shame; but with the humble is wisdom."
>
> Proverbs 13:10, "By pride comes nothing but strife, But with the well-advised is wisdom."
>
> Proverbs 16:18, "Pride goes before destruction, And a haughty spirit before a fall."
>
> Proverbs 29:23, "A man's pride will bring him low, But the humble in

spirit will retain honor."

(NKJV)

Just by looking at these few verses, we can see how pride causes issues. Pride will cause destruction, just ask those who have fallen due to pride. They will tell you that their pride and ego caused them to self-destruct. We can fight pride with humility and wisdom. We can also fight it with the help of Jesus Christ. That will help you keep your pride under control. We will look at wisdom more in depth in our next chapter.

Self-Centeredness

The other area of concern is self-centeredness. As leaders, we cannot become all about "me." The world does not revolve around you and neither does the success that your team creates. You have to get away from the "I did this…" and the "I created this…" mindset. You have to get the focus off of you and onto your team. They deserve the credit and the success that comes with accomplishment. As the leader, you have to stay humble and find the things in the success that you still need to work on. Even though the team succeeded, there is always something to improve on or something to learn from. Do not fall into the mindset that there is nothing to improve on when you and your team have a success.

Look at Alabama Head Coach Nick Saban. He is always looking for ways to improve his teams even though they are successful and they win championships. He stresses playing for 60 minutes and everyone doing their job. The little details and mistakes drive him crazy. Alabama was soundly in control of the BCS Championship Game against Notre Dame a few years ago and Coach Saban was still coaching and still looking for ways to improve. Never become so self-involved that you forget to learn.

Now that we have looked at pride and self-centeredness, we need to look at ways to combat them. We have seen that humility and wisdom help prevent these items, but I want to add two more. Those are self-discipline and self-control. Leaders must develop self-discipline and self-control to combat issues with ego. John C. Maxwell put it best when he said, "Discipline does not automatically make someone a leader, but no one can long remain a leader without it." Having these two items, will make it easier to fight your ego. You will be able to keep it in check by establishing discipline and control over your mental state.

Ego causes many problems to leaders and it does not always show up early in their career. Most times it shows up in the end of their career and causes it to come to a crashing end. In *The John C. Maxwell Leadership Bible*, John wrote a list that I wanted to include at the end of this chapter. It talks about why leaders fail in the end of their life:

"Many Leaders fail toward the end of their life because:

1. They somehow dilute the original vision that drove them
2. Their success distorts them
3. Their weaknesses go unaddressed (19)."

This completely explains the role ego plays in leadership failures. It is explained in points number 2 and 3. John C. Maxwell said, "Unaddressed cracks in character only get deeper and more destructive with time." Ego is a crack in your character and must be addressed daily in order to keep it from causing you to fail. Lily Tomlin wrote, "The road to success is always under construction." You always have to work on issues along the way to success. Never think you have arrived and always work on your ego. Your ego should always be under construction as you should always be working to control it. Be aware that it is a problem for all and understand what it can do if left unattended. Do not go down as a leader who let his or her ego dictate their ending.

SOLOMON

Solomon used wisdom to lead and make the best decisions.

Making decisions is a key responsibility for leaders. As a leader, you have to make many decisions daily. Making decisions is not always easy and that is where leaders struggle. Not all leaders have the experience needed to make the more difficult decisions that will arise. That is where wisdom and experience come into play. In order to make decisions, you have to use your wisdom and past experiences to make the right decisions. When it comes to wisdom, we can look at Solomon for the best example. Solomon is known as the wisest man to ever live and it showed during his leadership.

Solomon's experience with wisdom started in 2 Chronicles Chapter 1. This is when God appeared to him and asked what he needed. The passage goes as follows when starting at verse 7 and ending at verse 12:

> "On that night God appeared to Solomon, and said to him, "Ask! What shall I give you?" And Solomon said to God: "You have shown great mercy to David my father, and have made me king in his place. Now, O Lord God, let Your promise to David my father be established, for You have made me king over a people like the dust of the earth in multitude. Now give me wisdom and knowledge, that I may go out and come in before this people; for who can judge this great people of Yours?" Then God said to Solomon: "Because this was in your heart, and you have not asked riches or wealth or honor or the life of your enemies, nor have you asked for long life – but have asked wisdom and knowledge for yourself that you may judge My people over whom I have made you king – wisdom and knowledge are granted to you (NKJV).""

As we see from this passage of scripture, Solomon knew the importance of wisdom and the role it would play in his life. It was going to play a daily role in his life as King of Israel and he wanted to have the wisdom need to make the right decisions for God's people.

Before we move on, I want to take a quick moment to define wisdom so we have a better understanding of the concept of this chapter. Merriam-Webster's Dictionary defines wisdom as "knowledge that is gained by having many experiences in life

(20)." It is also defines as "the natural ability to understand things that most other people cannot understand (20)." Seeing wisdom defined now shows us that you can gain wisdom from experiences. That is the way most leaders gain wisdom. There are some people in life that have natural wisdom. That is a gift from God that most people will not have. So most of us will have to develop our wisdom.

Solomon knew he needed wisdom but did not have the time to gain it from experience. He was a king and was going to have to make decisions that affected a lot of people. He knew he needed wisdom from God. Unlike Solomon, most of us will gain wisdom thru our experiences. We will make decisions that are not always the correct ones and we will learn from it. John C. Maxwell said, "Experience is not the best teacher, evaluated experience is the best teacher." We gain wisdom thru our experiences but we will not gain much if we do not evaluate the experience to see what we need to learn.

Alexandre Dumas said, "All human wisdom is summed up in two words; wait and hope." We gain wisdom thru waiting on the experiences we need to teach us. We all have to learn from mistakes and failures. Those are the best teachers. Do not be afraid to make the wrong decisions. They will only help your wisdom grow stronger. Always look for the lesson behind all your experiences. This is best summed up by a quote from Vernon Sanders Law, "Experience is a hard teacher because she gives the test first, the lessons afterwards."

Like I said earlier, Solomon did not have time to gain wisdom from experience because he was king and had to judge his people. In this text judge means to make decisions. He was tested early in his years as king. This is seen in 1 Kings 3:16-28 when he had to make a wise judgment:

"Now two women who were harlots came to the king, and stood before him. And one women said, "O my lord, this woman and I dwell in the same house; and I gave birth while she was in the house. Then it happened, the third day after I had given birth, that this woman also gave birth. And we were together; no one was with us in the house, except the two of us in the house. And this woman's son died in the night, because she lay on him. So she arose in the middle of the night and took my son from my side, while your maidservant slept, and laid him in her bosom. And when I arose in the morning to nurse my son, there he was, dead. But when I examined him in the morning, indeed, he was not my son whom I had borne." Then the other woman said, "No! But the living one is my son, and the dead one is your son." And the first woman said, "No! But the dead one is your son, and the living one is my son." Thus they spoke before the king. And the king said,

"The one says, 'This is my son, who lives, and your son is the dead one'; and the other says, 'No! But your son is the dead one, and my son the living one.'" Then the king said, "Bring me a sword." So they brought a sword before the king. And the king said, "Divide the living child in two, and give half to one, and half to the other." Then the woman whose son was living spoke to the king, for she yearned with compassion for her son; and she said, "O my lord, give her the living child, and by no means kill him!" But the other said, "Let him be neither mine nor yours, but divide him." So the king answered and said, "Give the first woman the living child, and by no means kill him; she is his mother." And all Israel heard of the judgment which the king had rendered; and they feared the king, for they saw that the wisdom of God was in him to administer justice (NKJV)."

After this happened, all of Israel knew that Solomon was wise and that God had granted him wisdom. They knew he was going to be fair, just, and judge based on God. Solomon used his wisdom wisely and led his people appropriately until the end of his reign when he began to make mistakes.

Why is wisdom important? Wisdom is important because it helps us make the right decisions. As a leader it is extremely important to make the right decisions. If you do not make good decisions then it affects more than just you. It affects your team and many more people. You cannot make decisions without thinking them thru and making sure that you have looked at all options available. A lot rides on your decisions and your choices. Here are a few things that wisdom helps you do:

1. Make wise decisions
2. Choose the right people
3. Judge wisely
4. Recognize priorities
5. Gain perspective

Wisdom helps with these as well as many others that will arise during your leadership. As you see with those items, a lot rides on wisdom. That is why wisdom is important to us a leaders.

A lot of people think that gaining experience and gaining wisdom is a waste of time. But I tell you that it is not. Try to go thru life without experiences and see how things go for you. You cannot even get a job now a days without some kind of experience. So do you think someone can be a leader without some experience? The answer is no. As a leader you have to have experience that leads to gaining wisdom. Augusta Rodin said, "Nothing is a waste of time if you use the experience wisely."

Wisdom should be used for the good of your team not for the good of yourself. You should never try to gain self-satisfaction as a leader. This is true with wisdom. Do not use your wisdom and your experiences to gain self-satisfaction. This goes back to fighting your ego and not allowing yourself to benefit more than the team.

Solomon was wise but he allowed his ego to change his path. Solomon forgot who brought him to where he was and began to fall as a leader at the end of his reign. In the end, he was not as wise as he was at the beginning and it showed in how he led his people.

Johann Wolfgang von Goethe said, "Wisdom is found only in truth." Finally, to gain wisdom, you have to find and gain the truth. You will not uncover the wisdom needed from experiences if you do not find the truth in them.

To close out our chapter about wisdom, I want to include this passage from Proverbs 1:2-7:

> "To know wisdom and instructions,
> To perceive the words of understanding,
> To receive the instruction of wisdom,
> Justice, judgment, and equity;
> To give prudence to the simple,
> To the young man knowledge and discretion –
> A wise man will hear and increase learning,
> And a man of understanding will attain wise counsel,
> To understand a proverb and an enigma,
> The words of the wise and their riddles.

The fear of the Lord is the beginning of knowledge,

But fools despise wisdom and instruction (NKJV)."

Wisdom is important and should be a trait that you should strive for as a leader. Do not get discouraged when it does not come at first. You will have to work to gain wisdom. Just remember this from Ecclesiastes 10:10, "…But wisdom brings success (NKJV)."

DAVID

David exemplifies loyalty in the midst of crises.

Throughout this book we have covered many important qualities of a leader. But in my opinion none are as important as the one we will discuss now. It is said that the difference between good leadership and great leadership can be defined using a single word. That word is loyalty. Without loyalty a leader truly has nothing. Everything in leadership revolves around loyalty. That is the loyalty of the leader to the team and the loyalty of the team to the leader. Loyalty is a not a one way street – it is a two way street. It goes both ways.

Since loyalty is important, this chapter of the book may

seem short for such an important topic. It is short because it is very easy to show you the importance of loyalty. So, let's start by looking at our biblical leader example. It is not hard to see why I picked David as our loyalty example. David was extremely loyal in his leadership. We can see this throughout 1 Samuel. David was loyal to King Saul from the time he met him until the time he was anointed the next king, even when Saul was trying to kill him. David was so loyal to Saul that even when he had multiple chances to kill him, he did not. You really have to be loyal to someone in order to not kill them if they are trying to kill you. David was that loyal.

This is not the only example of loyalty when it comes to David. David was also loyal to Saul's son, Jonathan. While Saul was trying to find David, Jonathan was helping him hide and stay out of harm's way. David and Jonathan were friends and were loyal to each other. They were both risking life for each other. A true testament to loyalty. Loyalty is about being there for someone no matter what the risk, the cost, the issue, or the result. Loyalty is a true attribute of a servant leader.

Harvey Mackay said, "Employee loyalty begins with employer loyalty. Your employees should know that if they do the job they were hired to do with reasonable amount of competence and efficiency, you will support them." You may be saying – that quote does not have anything to do with leadership. Well, just wait a minute as I change a few words for you. Team loyalty starts with leader loyalty. Your team should know that if they do the work they were chosen to do to the best of their abilities that you will support them. That's the importance of loyalty to leadership.

So, what is loyalty? I think it is best defined by a quote from WWE Superstar, John Cena. Cena says, "When people show loyalty to you, you take care of those who are with you. It's how it goes with everything. If you have a small circle of friends, and one of those friends doesn't stay loyal to you, they don't stay your friend for very long." Loyalty is simply taking care of those you care about. Leaders care about their team, so they are loyal to their team. It also works the other way because members of the team should care for the leader and should be loyal to them. If there is someone on the team that is not loyal to you or the team, it is time to remove them from the team. If you do not, they will be a hindrance to the team.

Why is loyalty important? I have determined five reasons that loyalty is important. These are not in any particular order and we will discuss each one in detail momentarily:

1. Builds Trust
2. Builds Cohesiveness
3. Builds Common Bond
4. Builds Respect
5. Builds Teamwork

Now, let us look at each one.

Builds Trust

Loyalty helps build trust between the leader and the team. When the team sees that the leader is there for them and that he cares for them, trust is formed. It has been said that, "People do not care how much you know until they know how much you care." Being able to genuinely show your team that you care will show them that they can trust you. Trust is extremely important in leadership. That is why it goes hand in hand with loyalty. Without trust there is no loyalty.

Builds Cohesiveness

Loyalty build cohesiveness with the entire team. When people are loyal to each other they build cohesiveness and stick together. They do things together and talk to each other away from the team setting. They form relationships that help them build the cohesiveness needed to be a strong team. This cohesiveness forms not only between team members but also with the leader. With loyalty the "stickiness" that holds the team together is formed.

Builds Common Bond

Loyalty builds a common bond with the team. It helps establish the commonality needed to get the team going. It helps bring together the goals and the vision. It bonds them together and helps the team see the bond. Loyalty helps everyone get on the same page and join the common good for the team.

Builds Respect

Loyalty builds respect. Just like it builds trust, it builds respect. Everyone wants to be respected and it does not change in the team setting or the leadership setting. Respect is earned just like trust is earned. Being loyal to one another helps establish the respect needed. When people stick up for one another they ended up respecting each other because they know they will have each other's back.

Builds Teamwork

Finally, loyalty builds teamwork. When you have established the other four concepts, then you establish teamwork. Once a leader and their team trust each other, are cohesive, have a common bond, and respect each other; then they can establish teamwork. A team has to have those four things in order to actually work together. If one ingredient is missing, then so is the teamwork. These five items all work together to form the leader and the team and it is all thanks to loyalty.

In order to wrap up our chapter on loyalty, I want to give you a few more quotes to think about in terms of loyalty. These quotes are not entirely about leadership but they show us the importance of loyalty in all aspects of our lives. I think it is extremely important to think of loyalty in all aspects not just the leadership aspects. I know for one that I have struggled with loyalty and wish that I had been more loyal when I needed to be instead of backing down and shying away. We all make mistakes, but with loyalty we will have people there for us who will help us thru. Enjoy the quotes!

"I look for these qualities and characteristics in people. Honesty is number one, respect, and absolutely the third would have to be **loyalty**." – Summer Altice

"Success is the result of perfection, hard work, learning from failure, **loyalty**, and persistence." – Colin Powell

"The foundation stones for a balanced success are honesty, character, integrity, faith, love, and **loyalty**." – Zig Ziglar

DANIEL

Daniel used courage to do what was right even when it was uncommon to do so.

When we read through the book of Daniel, we see prime examples of courage in action. Courage is very important when it comes to leadership. Every decision that you make in leadership will not be easy. Some of those decisions will take courage in order for you to make them. Sometimes the decision will go against the status quo and will make people uneasy. Courage will be needed to make the decision. Sometimes the decision will be unpopular and will go against the majority of the team. Again, courage will be needed to make the decision. We can sit here and talk about the types of decisions you will make as a leader, but we do not need to do that for you to understand that courage will be needed in your daily leadership.

The Merriam-Webster Dictionary defines courage as "the ability to do something that you know is difficult or dangerous (21)." There will be a lot of difficult decisions that you will be required to make, you will need courage to make them. We can see courage in action when we look at the book of Daniel. There are actually two great examples of courage in the book. We will look at both in order to show how courage is important to a leader.

The first example comes from Shadrach, Meshach, and Abed-Nego in Daniel Chapter 3. When we read about them in this chapter, we see that they are facing a difficult decision. They have to decide rather to bow down to King Nebuchadnezzar or to keep their faith and not bow down. Most people would become fearful of the consequences of not bowing down; however, Shadrach, Meshach, and Abed-Nego did not. Their faith in God fueled their courage to not honor the King's commands. Faith is needed to help with the courage in our lives. Merriam-Webster Dictionary defines faith as the "strong belief or trust in someone or something (22)."

When we have faith (or a strong belief), then we have courage (or ability to act).

Shadrach, Meshach, and Abed-Nego used their faith and courage to not bow down to King Nebuchadnezzar. Then they had to face the consequences of disobedience. They were thrown into the Fiery Furnace where they were saved by God and no harm was done to them. As we can see if we use courage and faith to make the difficult decisions, then in the long-run success will come. We cannot be afraid to make the difficult decision even in the face of adversity or opposition.

James Neil Hollingworth said, "Courage is not the absence of fear, but rather the judgment that something else is more important than fear." Do not let fear make your decisions, use your courage to stand up to your fears. We are all fearful and we all have fears, but we also have a tool that can help us fight those fears. That tool is courage and faith.

Now, we can look at the second example in the book of Daniel which is Daniel himself. We read about Daniel's decision in

Chapter 6. Daniel was a just man of God and followed Him daily. God allowed Daniel to do great things due to his faith, which in turn made others jealous. Those jealous individuals plotted against Daniel and got King Darius to pass a law that would only allow people to worship himself. Once passed, Daniel continued to worship God and did so in public. He did not hide his faith even knowing he would be thrown in the Lion's Den. Daniel disobeyed King Darius' decree and was thrown in the Lion's Den. The next morning Daniel was found unharmed and safe. God protected him because Daniel used his faith to fuel his courage.

Our two examples showed how courage is used in difficult/dangerous situations/decisions. I know we may never face a situation as difficult or as dangerous as Daniel or as Shadrach, Meshach, and Abed-Nego. But we have to see how courage and our faith can help us in the time of need. As a leader, you will face those decisions. You will toss and turn at night, you will lose sleep, and you will wrestle with the pros and cons. But know that in the end having courage will help you make the right decision.

You may be asking what kind of decisions am I talking about

that will be difficult. Let me give you a few examples:

1. Terminating a Team Member
2. Promotions
3. Ethical Decisions
4. Decisions trying to break your trust with others
5. Changing the status quo

Those are a few of the decisions that I am talking about, but remember there are many others. I will not list them all because I know every leader will deal with their own set of difficult decisions plus I could leave some off. Just understand that you will face those difficult decisions and you will need help ensuring that you make the correct decision.

Courage is not easy to come by and not everyone uses it. If they did, the world would be a much better place. Ego, pride, and success get in the way of courage just like it does with other leadership characteristics. You have to work on using your courage. You have to understand that at first you will be mocked and ridiculed for using your courage to do the right thing but in the end it will get easier and people will ultimately see that you made the right decision. It will take time but they will see. I can honestly say that I have let fear get in the way of my courage and have made some bad decisions because of it, but I have bounced back from my mistakes and now use courage even if it is not popular to do so. You can turn your decision making around if you have lacked courage in the past but do not let it go for long or you will not be able turn your decisions around. Andrew Jackson said, "One man with courage makes a majority." That is how important courage is that if one person uses it, it will be noticed by all.

To wrap up our discussion on courage, I want to share some quotes about courage that sums up how important courage is in a leader's arsenal. Mary Anne Radmacher said, "Courage doesn't always roar. Sometimes courage is the quiet voice at the end of the day saying, 'I will try again tomorrow.'" Courage is quiet. You do not go around screaming that you have courage. It is not something that you show off. You use it to help you through the difficult times and use it to continue trying to make the best/right decisions.

Mark Twain said, "Courage is the resistance to fear, mastery of fear – not absence of fear." Just because you use courage does not mean that fear will completely go away. Fear will still be in the picture. Courage just helps keep the fear down and in its correct place which is not in the decision making process.

Finally, Eddie Rickenbacker said, "Courage is doing what you are afraid to do. There can be no courage unless you are scared." When you make these difficult decisions, you will be scared – that's the fear factor involved. Remember it is okay to be scared and afraid when making decisions. Courage is there to help make them easier because you know you are doing the right thing in the long run.

Courage is very important in a leader's world. You have to have it to help you thru your leadership journey. Remember that courageous decisions are better than popular decisions. Do not be scared to make that courageous decision. In the long run, you will be glad you did. It may not be today, it may not be tomorrow, but soon you will see the fruits of that decision. I will leave you with this closing statement about courage by Ralph Waldo Emerson:

"Whatever you do, you need

courage

whatever course you

decide upon, there is always

someone to tell you that

you are wrong.

There are always

difficulties arising that

tempt you to believe your

critics are right.

To map out a course of

action and follow it to an

end requires some of the

same courage that a soldier

needs."

ESTHER

Esther sacrifices her position to help her people.

There are a lot of characteristics, skills, and qualities that leaders need to possess. The topic of this chapter is one that is hard for a lot of leaders to grasp and understand. Leaders must be able to sacrifice. Sacrifice is a big element to being a successful leader. We have the opportunity to learn from a leader that had to decide if she would sacrifice her leadership. Esther is a great example of how a leader must sacrifice to be successful. Esther was put in a tough situation and had to make a tough choice.

When we look in the book of Esther, we see that the king has made a decree to destroy the Jews, including Mordecai – Esther's uncle. Esther was the Queen at this time. The king was not aware

that Esther was a Jew when the decree was made. Mordecai

confronted Esther about helping her people. The discussion is seen

in Esther 4:11-16:

> ""All the king's servants and the people of the king's provinces know that any man or woman who goes into the inner court to the king, who has not been called, he has but one law: put all to death, except the one to whom the king holds out the golden scepter, that he may live. Yet I myself have not been called to go in to the king these thirty days." So they told Mordecai Esther's words. And Mordecai told them to answer Esther: "Do not think in your heart that you will escape in the king's palace any more than all the other Jews. For if you remain completely silent at this time, relief and deliverance will arise for the Jews from another place, but you and your father's house will perish. Yet who knows whether you have come to the kingdom for such a time as this?" Then Esther told them to reply to Mordecai: "Go, gather all the Jews who are present in Shushan, and fast for me; neither eat or drink for three days, night or day. My maids and I will fast likewise. And so I will go to the king, which is against the law; and if I perish, I perish (NKJV)!""

Esther had to make the ultimate sacrifice for her people and face

the possibility of death. Esther sacrificed her livelihood for her

people and in the end we see that Esther was successful in saving

the Jews – thanks to her willingness to sacrifice her own life.

As a leader, we may not have to sacrifice our life but we will

have to make sacrifices to be successful. Merriam-Webster

Dictionary defines sacrifice as "the act of giving up something that you want to keep especially in order to get to do something else or to help someone (23)." Leaders have to sacrifice in order to go higher in their leadership. John C. Maxwell wrote "The Law of Sacrifice" in his book *The 21 Irrefutable Laws of Leadership*. The "Law of Sacrifice" says that "a leader must give up to go up (24)." This law states why sacrifice is important to leaders. You have to give up things in order to continue going up your leadership ladder.

Another concept that shows how sacrifice is important is The Leadership Pyramid (25). The Leadership Pyramid shows us that as you rise in leadership, responsibilities increase and rights decrease.

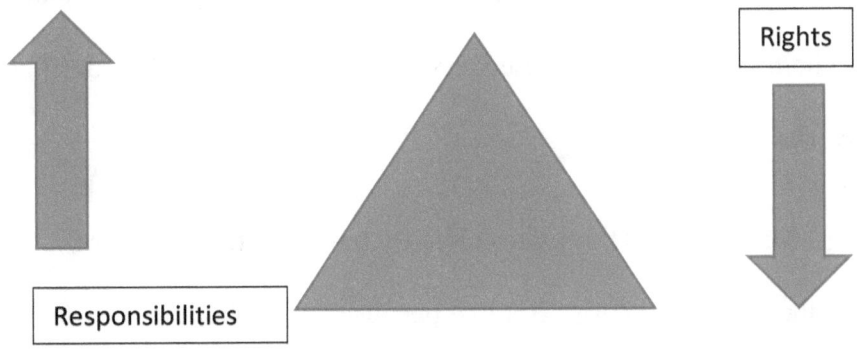

Using the diagram above, you can have a visual image of The Leadership Pyramid and see how it works. Once again, you can see that as your responsibilities as a leader increase (or rise) then your rights as a leader decrease (or fall). You may now be asking what "rights" will a leader lose or have decrease. Here is a list of a few, but there are many more:

1. Privacy
2. Free Time/Hobbies
3. Friends
4. Family Time
5. Health/Well Being
6. Relaxation/Peace of Mind
7. Money
8. Promotions

A leader is always on call and may be needed at a moment's notice. John C. Maxwell said, "Leadership means sacrifice." Being a leader means that you will sacrifice in order to be successful and to help your people. The Leadership Pyramid shows how sacrifice works for a leader.

Many leaders throughout history have had to make sacrifices on their way to the top. But just because you make it to the top does not mean that you are done sacrificing. John C. Maxwell says, "Sacrifice is an ongoing process, not a one-time payment." As a leader you will constantly make sacrifices in order to go up in leadership. Your team will learn to continually respect you for the sacrifices that you make. Your team will see your sacrifices and gain the following for you as their leader:

- Respect
- Trust
- Loyalty

Sacrifice is a key to leadership and is seen in its everyday actions. It helps in building relationships with your team and with producing results with your team.

Lou Holtz once said, "The freedom to do your own thing ends when you have obligations and responsibilities." As a leader, you will have many obligations and responsibilities. You will sacrifice your own things when those obligations and responsibilities arise. Leadership is not easy and that can be seen through the things we have to sacrifice. If sacrificing was easy, everyone would do it. But it's not easy. It is very difficult to sacrifice things that you love and have passion for. As a leader, you should have passion for your people which in turn will help make the sacrifices worth it. Sacrificing for your team will help you as you develop them to become leaders.

I have had my opportunities to sacrifice in order to help my team. I have passed on opportunities to further my career goals in order to help my team. As a leader, I felt like I needed to stay where I was in order to benefit my team. I felt like I needed to be there to continue developing those around me. I know I pushed myself back on my goals, but I feel that because I did I helped others develop into better leaders which in turn will help them in their futures. As a leader we should want to develop our team even if it means sacrificing our career goals. I believe that because I did this, that my leadership actually increased and I was benefitted because of my sacrifice.

Another way I have sacrificed is by sacrificing for my personal growth in order to help others. As a leader, we must always grow and continue to learn. Leadership is an ongoing process and you have to grow or you will be left behind. I also use the lessons I learn from personal growth to teach my team, but it is not always easy to gather these resources. Learning more about leadership can be expensive but you have to sacrifice in other areas of your life in order to grow. In the long run, it will be worth the sacrifice.

Those are just a few examples to show you how I have sacrificed. I do not believe it would be fair to write a chapter on sacrifice if I did not share examples in my own life. Do not be afraid to make sacrifices. I know it will not be easy at first, but just know that it will be worth the hardships in the end. All great leaders make sacrifices for their people. It's a key to leadership and a key to being a respected leader.

THE GOOD SAMARITAN

The Good Samaritan shows how a leader should care about their people.

Most of this book has taught us leadership qualities from biblical leaders. However, during his teachings Jesus used parables to exemplify qualities of Christians. While reading thru the Bible, one parable that stood out to me as an example of leadership was the parable of The Good Samaritan. Jesus taught the parable of The Good Samaritan in the book of Luke. So, I want to take a different perspective in this chapter and teach a leadership quality using a parable instead of a biblical leader. I personally believe that the parable of The Good Samaritan shows us the quality of caring at its best. As a leader, we must care for our people. If we do not, they will leave us for a leader who will. Before we go in depth about caring, let us look at the parable first. The parable of The Good Samaritan is found in Luke 10:30-37:

> "Then Jesus answered and said: "A certain man went down from Jerusalem to Jericho, and fell among thieves, who stripped him of his clothing, wounded him, and departed, leaving him half dead. Now by chance a certain priest came down that road. And when he saw him, he passed by on the other side. Likewise a Levite, when he arrived at the place, came and looked, and passed by on the other side. But a certain Samaritan, as he journeyed, came where he was. And when he saw him, he had compassion. So he went to him and bandaged his wounds, pouring oil and wine; and he set him on his own animal, brought him to an inn and took care of him. On the next day, when he departed, he took out two denarii, gave them to the inn-keeper, and said to him, 'Take care of him; and whatever more you spend, when I come again, I will repay you.' So which of these three do you think was neighbor to him who fell among the thieves?" And he said, "He who showed mercy on him." Then Jesus said to him, "Go and do likewise (NKJV).""

This parable shows a man who took care of another man he did not know. He had compassion for him and his situation. If a stranger can care for an individual that he does not know, then how can a leader not care for a person that they do know?

Caring is another key quality of a leader. A leader has to care for his people and he must be genuine in doing so. People know the difference between sincere caring and insincere caring. A leader cannot play a game when it comes to caring for their people.

Leaders develop relationships with their team. It's a common practice in the leadership world. One way the leaders do this is by showing that they care for the individuals that they lead. Caring and relationships are so important in leadership that John C. Maxwell included this as one of *The Five Levels of Leadership.* It is officially called "Level 2 – Permission." One key concept from this level is that "You can't lead people until you like people (26)." If you do not like your people, then you will never care for them. If they have the sense that you do not care for them, then they will not develop relationships with you and in time they will leave you as their leader.

So you may be asking yourself, how do I show I care as a leader? There are many ways that you can show your people that you care. We will discuss them in the next few parts of this chapter. The ways are as follows:

Listen

The first way that you can show people you care is by listening. Everyone needs to be heard at some point. Being a leader that listens and that lends a listening ear shows that you have concern for your people and that you care about them. People need someone who will listen to them. Everyone goes thru tough times and needs someone they can count on to hear them. A lot of the time they go to their leader for support and to talk. That is when we as leaders must step up and lend the ear they need. We need to be there to listen and help them through their situation. Showing your people that you will listen will show them that you care and will help you develop relationships with them.

Empathy

Merriam-Webster's Dictionary defines empathy as "the feeling that you understand and share another person's experiences and emotions: the ability to share someone else's feelings (27)." Empathy goes a long way in leadership. Your people want to know that you understand them and that you share the same sentiments as they do. They want to share experiences with you. Empathy shows you care. Showing you understand them and that you share emotions with them leads to building a caring atmosphere in your leadership.

Trust

Trust is the third way that you can show your people that you care. Trusting in your team shows them that you have complete faith in their abilities. It shows them that you trust them to make decisions in regards to the organization, the goal, and the vision. It gives them that extra push they need to succeed. A team that is not trusted will not succeed. They will cower because they will be afraid to make decisions even if they are good decisions. You have to trust your people in order to care for them.

Loyalty

Loyalty shows your people that you will stick by them no matter what comes along the way. It shows them that you will be there for them and that you will be by their side. Loyalty means a lot to the team. It means that they know you have their back in all situations. They know that no matter what decision is made that you will be there for them. They know they can take risk in achieving the success that they are trying to reach because you will be there even if they make a bad decision.

Inclusion

The fifth way that you can show your people that you care is by inclusion. Inclusion is simply including them. You can include them in decision making, brainstorming, vision making, etc. There are many more ways that you can include your team members. The main thing to remember is to include them. That is all they want. They want to be included in all aspects of the team. Inclusion shows them that they are valued by you.

Commitment

Commitment is another way that you can show your team that you care. Your team needs to know that you are committed to them as a team and as individuals. Commitment shows that you are committed to them for the long run. Your people want to know that you are behind them supporting them and that you are committed to them. They do not want a leader that is constantly looking for the next big thing and that when they find it they are going to jump ship. Leaders that are committed to their team have easier times building relationships with their team.

Add Value

The final way that we will look at, to show your people you care, is by adding value. When you add value to people it shows that you want to help them grow. One of the best ways to show you care is by helping people grow in order to reach their goals. Growth is key to success and being able to add value to people helps them grow. A leader should always want to add value to their team. As a leader, you should want your people to grow and be better than you are. You should want to teach them everything that you can. You should promote an atmosphere of growth. If you do this, then you will add value to them.

The seven items above are just a few ways you can show your people that you care. I believe that they are the most important ways to do so. If you incorporate all of them, then you will show your people and team that you care for them and that you want to establish relationships with them. Your people are the key to your success. You need them to succeed. In order to keep them happy, you have to establish relationships with them. You have to learn what motivates them, what makes them tick, and what their goals are. You cannot be afraid to develop relationships with your people and you cannot be afraid to show them that you care. John C. Maxwell said it best when he said, "People do not care how much you know until they know how much you care." That statement says it all. You can know everything in the world and be a walking encyclopedia, but if you do not care – it is all for nothing. All people want is to know that they are cared for.

The most successful leaders know that relationships and caring is the key to success. They know that their people and their team are their best assets. They know that they have to build relationships with their people. Finally, they know that caring is the key that keeps all of it together. If a stranger can care for a hurting individual that he had never met before, then we as leaders can care for the people that we see every day. Leaders do not have to be stand-offish. They do not have to stand above everyone. They do not have to be all high and mighty. They have to be caring people. It is as simple as that. Be a caring leader and watch your relationships grow and watch your people become more successful.

If you think you will have a problem caring then listen closely to what Dr. Seuss once said. He said, "Unless someone like you cares a whole awful lot, nothing is going to get better. Its not." Caring makes everything better. It opens up doors and it will open up doors in your leadership. If you already show your people that you care then you can testify that what I have talked about is true. People work harder for someone who cares for them. They work harder for people they have developed relationships with. I know this from experience. I have seen it every day in my leadership journey. I have practiced it both ways with my people and my team and I can tell you without any doubt that caring for your people is a key to leadership and the key to success for all involved. People leave leaders not organizations. If you are losing a lot of people, then you need to look at yourself. I bet when you do, you will see that you do not sincerely care for your people. Take the example of The Good Samaritan and care for people.

PAUL

Saul's transformation to Paul shows how change is needed in a leader's life.

The last characteristic that I want to share with you in this book is that of change. Change is extremely important when it comes to leadership. This is because everything changes and nothing stays the same. You must always be ready to lead change. Even though we know everything changes, people still fear and resist it. We, as leaders, must be ready to lead that change in a variety of ways. That's what we will talk about in this chapter.

First, I want to talk about why I chose Paul as the leader for this chapter. When reading thru the book of Acts, it became clear to me that Paul was the obvious choice as the leader who best exemplified change. He went through a change that people do not regularly go thru. He completely changed himself when God spoke to him on the road to Damascus. Before that he was Saul. He was a leader against the Christian movement and he persecuted them. Then on the road to Damascus, God spoke to him and changed his heart and changed him to Paul. Paul then became a great leader of the church. He preached the gospel, witnessed, and led the church all in the name of the Lord. Saul's change to Paul was a complete 360 degree change and it shows us that change is necessary.

Why is change necessary? Change is needed because nothing ever stays the same. Life is constantly changing and evolving. If we do not change, then we will be left behind and of course fall behind. We cannot continue to lead people if we do not change because we cannot lead our people to success if we stay at the status quo level. People who do not change, stay at the same level and they eventually fall off. A great example of staying at status quo is with sports. Think of the teams that win championships versus teams that finish last. If you notice, most teams that win championships stay at the top while those at the bottom stay at the bottom. Do you know why? It's because the teams at the top change and evolve to continue to stay at the top while teams at the bottom do not evolve. They stay the same.

As I write this chapter, I myself am going thru a major change that I wanted to share in order to help show how change is needed. I recently received a promotion to become a Store Director. This means I have to leave the store that I have been working at for over eight and move to another store. This also means that I have to leave a city that I have lived in for over eleven years. I am going thru professional and personal change. These changes are not easy. I have grown to love the community that I am leaving and I have developed many friendships that I will be leaving. I also know that I will be leaving a team that I have developed and mentored for years. While the change is going to be tough on me, it will be equally tough on them. It is hard for a leader to leave their team but sometimes it is necessary to do so. Sometimes as a leader, you have to leave your team because you have taken them as far as you can. It is never easy but it is necessary. John F. Kennedy said it best when he said, "Change is the law of life and those who look only to the past or present are certain to miss the future."

When change requires us to leave as leaders, it effects three groups of people. First, it affects the leader, then it affects the "old" team, and finally it affects the "new" team. Obviously, we know how it affects the leader based on what I shared with you above. The main part I want to focus on here is how it affects the teams. It affects them both in the same ways. They have to lose their leader and deal with those emotions. They then gain a new leader and have to deal with those emotions. They have to then learn and develop a new relationship with the new leader. They have to learn to trust the new leader. It takes time for the two teams to transition during this change.

How can we as the leader help make the transition easier? The following are a few steps that I feel can be used to help with the change transition. These can be used with all types of change, not just the change of leaving your team. I just used that as the primary example because I am going thru it at this time.

1. Always talk to your team about change.
2. Prepare your team for the upcoming change.

3. Ensure that you answer any questions regarding the change.
4. Have one-on-one discussions if needed.
5. Lead the change.
6. Continue to meet with your team until all are comfortable with the change.
7. Summarize the successes/failures of the change once it is complete with your team.
8. Learn from the successes/failures before your next change occurs.

Now, we will look more in depth at each of these steps for change transition.

Always Talk to Your Team About Change:

The first step you need to take as a leader is to always talk to your team about change. Teach them about change and help them learn the effects of change. Talking about change with your team will help them whenever change finally occurs. This will make it easier on all especially you as the leader as you champion the change when it comes. Just as you teach your team about leadership, attitude, and many more skills; change is also something that you want to teach in order to learn more about it.

Prepare Your Team for the Upcoming Change:

Once you know that change is going to occur, you need to prepare your team for it. This means having meetings with your team to talk about what is going to occur. It also means having one-on-one discussions with all involved. This will help because everyone will have questions but some people may be fearful to discuss them in a group setting. Once you have done these items, I encourage you to continue to have meetings with your teams to discuss the change. This includes before, during, and after.

Ensure That You Answer Any Questions Regarding the Change:

We all know that questions are going to arise when change is about to happen. As a leader, you need to do your research and be prepared to answer any questions that will come your way. Always remember that if you do not know the answer to the question that it is okay to say you do not know but you will find out. You are better off finding an answer rather than trying to talk your way through it. This will only cause fear among your team if they find out that you really did not know the answer. Another good practice would be to publish a newsletter with questions and answers that arise. Remember, one person may ask the question but all will probably be thinking of it as well.

Have One-On-One Discussions if Needed:

I noted this earlier in the second step but it is extremely important and is its own step. Having team meetings are important but it is equally important to have one-on-one meetings. People are going to have questions and fears about the change that they will not want to discuss in front of others. It is important to have an "Open Door" during this time in order for your team to come talk to you about their fears and concerns. Let me make a quick side note before we move on. It is important for a leader to always have an "Open Door." You do not want to give the impression that you are off limits or unapproachable.

Lead the Change:

This may be one of the harder steps but it is also one of the most important. As the leader, you must lead the change. You have to be the one that leads the way. If at any point your team feels that you fear the change or that you are not behind the change, they will be reluctant to pursue the change. This will then make the change difficult and it will be met with resistance. Always be mindful that your team is watching and they will follow your lead. If you lead the change, they will accept it and they will embrace it. If you do not lead the change, they will fight it and never embrace it.

Continue to Meet With Your Team Until All Are Comfortable With the Change:

Just because the change is here does not mean that your job as the leader is done. There will be times that you will still have to lead the change and make sure that your team is adjusting to the change. It will be important to continue to meet with them until all are comfortable with the change and that the change has been embraced 100%. This could take a few weeks up to a few months. That will depend on the nature of the change. The important thing is to meet with them continually until you are without a doubt that the change has been successful.

Summarize the Successes/Failures of the Change Once it is Complete With Your Team:

As a leader, you will want to summarize the successes and the failures of the change that your team just went through. This is important on many levels. First, it is important because it will help you fix any failures with the change. Second, it will help you know what went well and what did not when the next change occurs.

Third, it gives your team a chance to give input about the process of implementing the change and the change itself. It is always good to take the time to reflect on how things went in different situations. Going thru a change is no different. I read a quote that fits here that I want to share. It was from an unknown person, "In the midst of change we find seed for the future." This is why you summarize what occurred with your team. You are looking toward the future.

Learn From the Successes/Failures Before Your Next Change Occurs:

The final step in the change process that I have shared with you is always important. As a leader, you need to ensure that you learn from the success and failures of the change. We have all heard that experience is the best teacher, but I agree with John C. Maxwell when he said, "Evaluated experience is the best teacher." You cannot learn from experience if you do not evaluate it. You have to know what went right and what went wrong. You have to look for the lessons involved and learn from it. Change is an experience and you have the chance to learn from it. Make sure you do. The more you learn from each change experience, the better leading the change will get for you.

As we close this chapter, I hope that you see that change is a must in life but that we do not have to be fearful of it. We just need to embrace it, lead it, and learn from it just as Saul did when he changed to Paul. Change will always be a part of leadership whether we want to admit it or not. That is why I felt that this chapter would be beneficial for us all. In closing, I will share an anonymous quote. "Change is the essence of life. Be willing to surrender what you are for what you could become."

As you get ready to turn the page to the next chapter, I am excited that we will get the chance to learn from the greatest leader of all time. This book would not be complete if we did not learn from the leadership of Jesus. I hope you are as excited to read the next chapter as I was to write it. Jesus gave us all the examples of leadership that we need and we will see that next.

JESUS

Jesus gives us the picture of the ultimate leader.

Throughout each of our previous chapters, we have discussed a biblical leader and a leadership quality that each one exhibited. During this chapter, we will learn how Jesus possessed all the qualities that we have discussed. Jesus gives us the picture of the ultimate leader by possessing all the leadership qualities that a leader needs. I consider Him the greatest leader to ever live. With that, we should easily be able to learn from His leadership and then be able to use that knowledge in our leadership. As you read through the books of Matthew, Mark, Luke, and John; you will be able to see the leadership of Jesus in action. As we discuss His leadership in the next few pages, remember that there are many other leadership qualities that Jesus possessed. I am just reflecting on the ones that I have included in this book. I hope that this chapter can help tie together everything we have discussed thus far. We will discuss each quality in the order that they appeared in the book.

Commitment

As you read in Matthew, Mark, Luke, and John; you can easily see Jesus' commitment. He was committed to God's Plan to save the human race. He was committed to making sure that the plan was carried out. Even when times got tough and Jesus was closer to the crucifixion, He was still committed to carrying out the plan. Jesus was also committed to teaching the Word of God and to His disciples. Jesus gave us the perfect example of commitment and how we should apply it to our leadership. We should never waiver from our commitment no matter how tough times get. Our followers want to know that we are committed to the cause and if we waiver from that commitment then we will lose them. Just think what would have happened if Jesus would not have been committed to God's Plan.

Adversity

Jesus went through a lot of adversity during his time on Earth. There are many examples that we could look at when it comes to adversity in His life. While reading Matthew 4:1-11, I decided that this would be the best example. This scriptures refers to Satan tempting Jesus. Satan came at Jesus three times to tempt Him while He was fasting and praying. Each time that Satan tried to tempt Jesus, he failed. Jesus faced the adversity from Satan and continued living His life and staying on track with the plan that God gave him. Adversity comes in many shapes and sizes and it may not always be easy to spot. Just remember that we will all face adversity in our leadership journey. We just have to stay true to our calling in order to face it and pass it. In the end, adversity makes us and our leadership stronger.

Vision

There are many visions that occurred during Jesus' time. Jesus presented visions to all during His ministry. He kept painting pictures of the future for all people. He had visions for His disciples as it related to carrying on the ministry and of the great sacrifice that He would be making. He also presented visions to the followers of his ministry as well as those that did not believe such as the Pharisees. Matthew 9:35-10:5 shows us the vision that God gave Him for the world. Visions are important because they help give our teams goals for the future. It also lets them know that we have a plan and that we know where we want to head. Without a vision, you have no purpose. Visions give us reason and give us purpose. They give us the needed direction to stay on track to success. Another vision that Jesus gave us is presented in Matthew 28:19-20 and is referred to as "The Great Commission." After Jesus arose from the dead, He had another vision that He wanted to give the disciples both present and future. He knew His earthly time was up but still needed to give a vision to those He left on Earth to carry on the Plan.

Communication

Communication is very important in leadership just as it is in any aspect of life. You have to be able to communicate with people in order to reach them. Jesus did this very well as He was able to reach many people during His leadership. Jesus used many ways to communicate with people but my favorite was His use of Parables.

Jesus used Parables to communicate many things to people. They

were used to teach principles, behaviors, and qualities that people

needed to possess. Jesus was able to connect to the individuals that

followed Him because of His communication. All of us

communicate; however, we all do not connect. It is important that

we connect with our teams when we communicate. Jesus

connected and He still does today.

Momentum

Momentum is very important when it comes to leadership. We

saw how momentum worked in Joshua's leadership. Jesus also had

momentum on His side during His ministry. Many people followed

Him to learn and to receive healing. He kept building momentum

with people as multitudes began to follow Him to listen and learn.

His momentum created spite in the hearts of the Pharisees because

they began to fear Jesus. Without positive momentum in Jesus'

leadership, He would not have been able to fulfill God's Plan.

Momentum created the needed spite to ensure that the plan was

followed. We all will need momentum to get us going as leaders in order to reach our vision and our goals. Momentum helps carry you along as a leader and gives you a needed boost at times. You can rely on momentum to carry you thru when times get tough and it also creates credibility for you as a leader.

Listening

We can read many times in the Bible where Jesus listened. Jesus listened to all who needed an ear. He listened to what they needed and He responded appropriately. Sometimes He listened and knew that He did not need to respond. Knowing when to respond and when not to respond is hard to learn. There is not a training manual for listening training. You have to develop this over time. There are many times that our people will come to us for a listening ear and as leaders we need to be there as the needed ear. Leading is not all about talking. Sometimes you have to be silent and listen.

Influence

As we learned earlier from a quote from John C. Maxwell, "Leadership is influence." Jesus was able to influence many during His ministry. When reading Matthew 4:12-25, we read about Jesus beginning His ministry. This set of scriptures shows us the beginning of Jesus' influence. There are many more examples of influence during Jesus' ministry, but showing where His influence starts is important. Influence is not given, it is earned. You do not automatically start with influence over people, you have to earn that. Jesus had to do the same. He earned His influence through His leadership.

Wisdom

Jesus exhibited wisdom at a very young age. In Luke 2:41-52, we see that Jesus was twelve years old and He was teaching the scholars of the church. Jesus was wise beyond His years. God gave Him wisdom at a very early age to ensure that He was able to fulfill the plan. While Jesus had wisdom, He also always used it for good. He never used His wisdom for personal gain or to wrong anyone. Wisdom is a powerful tool but it must also be used correctly. We must use the wisdom we gain as leaders to benefit others and not ourselves.

Loyalty

Loyalty is not a quality that is used as often as it should be. Loyalty seems to be a lost quality of leadership. Leaders have decided that being loyal makes them weak, so they jump ship often so they do not have to exhibit loyalty. Let me tell you that they are completely wrong. Loyalty is very much still needed today and we see that Jesus exhibited loyalty throughout His leadership. Jesus was loyal to all. In Luke 9:10-17, Jesus was loyal to the multitude that followed Him that day. Instead of sending them away, He kept them there and fed them. He fed 5,000 people with 5 loaves and 2 fishes. He showed them loyalty by feeding them and keeping them safe. They were loyal to Him, so He in turn was loyal to them. Jesus was also loyal to His disciples. Two distinct examples cross my mind here. Jesus was loyal to Judas even though He knew that Judas would betray Him. Jesus was also loyal to Peter even after Peter denied him three times. Jesus was loyal to people even in the bad times. That is the true mark of a leader. Being loyal is easy when things are good, but not so much when things are bad. We have to be loyal through every situation.

Courage

Courage is very important for a leader. We all must exhibit courage at times in our leadership journey. At times the decisions we make will not always be the most popular and we will need something to put us over the top to ensure we make that right decision. That is when courage arrives. In Matthew 26: 36-46, Jesus had to use courage to make it through the next decision He had to face. The scripture references the "Prayer in the Garden." Jesus was praying to see if there was any other way to save mankind rather than Him dying. Jesus had to then use courage to continue with God's Plan. Jesus used courage to continue on the journey and to face His betrayal and ultimately His crucifixion.

Sacrifice

When we talk about sacrifice, it is very easy to see the example that we will use here for Jesus. Matthew 27: 27-56 gives us the details of the crucifixion of Jesus. Jesus made the ultimate sacrifice for all of us when He died on the cross. Jesus showed us that there are times when we have to make sacrifices for the better. If Jesus would not have made this sacrifice for us, then we would not have the chance to see eternal life in Heaven. As leaders, we will have to make sacrifices in order to obtain success and reach the vision. Sacrifice is not to be taken lightly and is not always easy. You will struggle with sacrifice as a leader. Just remember that sacrifices are needed and will lead to better things in the future.

Caring

Jesus was a very caring leader. He cared about all mankind. He was a servant leader and did what He could to take care of people. He did this by teaching, preaching, and healing. He wanted to take care of all and this is seen by Him coming to Earth to make the ultimate sacrifice so that we could all be saved from our sins. Being a servant leader is a key but it does not happen overnight. It takes time to learn to serve and to do so in a humble manner. As humans, we are not wired to serve and be humble. As a leader, we have to work on that in order for us to be servant leaders. You cannot care for your people if you are prideful and boastful. You have to be humble.

Change

The last quality that we will look at is change. Change is a staple of life and will always occur. This was no different for Jesus. Jesus had to face change and lead change. Luke 2:30-32 best exemplifies change for Jesus. It says:

> "For my eyes have seen Your salvation, Which You have prepared before the face of all peoples, a light to bring revelation to the Gentiles, and the glory of Your people Israel (NKJV)."

Until I heard my dad preach on these verses, I was having trouble thinking of a good example for change for Jesus. But during his sermon it all fell into place. Dad preached on Jesus and change using the above verses and he said one thing that stuck with me. He said, "Jesus came to change the world." That's the greatest example ever. Jesus was sent here to change the world and He did just that. Some people feared the change and others embraced it. Whether they feared or embraced it, it happened. Jesus changed the world through His leadership and God's Plan.

Jesus exhibited all the qualities of a leader and led as only He could. He is and always will be the greatest leader to ever walk the face of this Earth and we should learn all we can from the

examples that He set. I hope that you enjoyed seeing how Jesus

exemplifies true leadership and the qualities of a leader.

UNLIKELY LEADERS

God calls unlikely leaders into leadership action.

To wrap up this book on leadership, I want to take a few moments to talk about unlikely leaders. I spoke briefly on this in our chapter about Gideon, but I wanted to share more in closing. As we have seen with the many leaders we have learned from, God calls unlikely leaders into leadership. God uses unknown people to become leaders and to do great things for Him and His kingdom.

There is an old leadership debate about whether leaders are born or made. This debate has been going on for years and will probably be going on for many more years to come. Based on my years of studying leadership, I can honestly say that leaders are made. I believe people are called into leadership. Once you realize your leadership calling, you use many ways to develop yourself which in turn means you are made. So a true leader is made. I am sure there will be plenty of people out there that will read this and disagree. I am completely fine with that because one must make up their own decision in regards to this argument.

There are many things you can do to "make" yourself a leader once you receive/recognize your calling. These include:

1. Read Books
2. Attend Workshops
3. Obtain a Mentor
4. Watch Videos/DVDs
5. Attend Seminars
6. Receive Training (i.e. job related)
7. Trial and Error (experience)

There are many more tools available to grow yourself as a leader – to make yourself better and more successful.

Now that we have that premise out of the way, we can focus on the main point of this chapter. That point involves "Unlikely Leaders." You are probably wondering… What is an Unlikely Leader? We are going to discuss that in detail over the next few paragraphs. To start that discussion, I want to open with one statement. At the beginning point of our leadership journey when we recognize our calling, we were all unlikely leaders. No one would have pointed at us and said, "You are a leader." Look at all the leaders we discussed in this book. Before God called them, no one would have said they were leaders. No one looked at George Washington or Abraham Lincoln in their youth and said that they were leaders. They had to develop into that role. We all have to have a starting point to our leadership journey. Each of us can look back in our lives and recall that point. I will share mine later in this chapter.

When studying the leaders of *The Bible*, we can see that all of them were "Unlikely Leaders." God chose people to become leaders that He could develop and use for good. Seeing people become leaders is a joy for leaders. It is what all of our goals should be. We should want to develop more leaders. That's what God did. He developed leaders in His image to do what He needed at that time. You might not realize it, but He is still doing that today. God is still developing leaders. He is still calling us to do

His work and to help lead His people. No matter if you are religious or not, God called you to leadership and made you an "Unlikely Leader."

Why does God chose "Unlikely Leaders?" He does so because we are easier to develop and guide. Leaders have to be developed to reach their potential. Calling an "Unlikely Leader" means that the development will be easier. It is easier to develop someone who is willing, than someone who thinks they have already arrived. Every leader we have discussed in this book fits that description even if they fought back at first. God used them to exhibit a characteristic that we all need to learn.

Think about your past. How you grew up. The type of student you were. Did you honestly think that you were destined to be a leader? Probably not. Truthfully, it was probably far from your mind. I was born to two wonderful parents that God so richly blessed me with – David and Joy Elliott – in a small south Alabama town of Bradley. I grew up in a God fearing home and family on a small farm. And I am so thankful I did. I was taught very valuable life lessons that I will never forget. I worked on the farm and went to school. I took my studies very serious and did not play sports like my friends. I was voted to leadership positions in High School due to having friends not because of my abilities. It was at that point that I was curious about leadership and began studying it. It was then that I realized my calling to be a leader. I knew at that point I was going to be a leader but I did not know why or what I would be called to do.

After High School, I attended college and continued to study leadership. I studied leadership using the ways I listed earlier in this chapter. It was not until after I graduated college and began my first job that I realized my leadership calling. My calling has been to develop other leaders. It's a calling that I have been very excited about and have been doing since I realized it. I have been developing leaders in my current job for over 8 years but I still felt that I was supposed to do more. That is when I realized that God wanted me to help others reach their leadership calling by writing this book. I have never written a book before but have felt that this was the plan for my leadership.

Now that I have shared a little more about me, I want you to use the included lines to write down your journey to leadership. You can be as lengthy or as brief as you need. This will be for you to use to remember where you came from. If you have not realized your leadership calling, remember where this is so you can write it down when you do. You will always want to remember when you got your calling.

_____

_____

_____

_____

_____

_____

_____

_____

_____

_____

Now, do you see how we are "Unlikely Leaders?" God has a special calling for all of us and it includes leadership. We have looked at examples of great biblical leaders throughout this book as well as the example of the greatest leader of all time – Jesus Christ, but there are many more in *The Bible* that we did not discuss. I encourage you to take time and learn about the other leaders as well. I hope that this book has encouraged you and helped make your leadership better. It has been a blessing for me to write it as I have taken a deeper look at my leadership to be a better leader and a better person. I will leave you with one final quote in closing,

"Don't be afraid to be amazing." – Andy Offutt Irwin

CONCLUSION

We have now had the opportunity to read and learn lessons on leadership by looking at the examples of fourteen biblical leaders. We were able to see good qualities as well as a bad quality. I hope that you can take each lesson and apply it to your leadership and that you can in turn teach it to your team in order to strengthen their leadership. Growing is a key to leadership. I hope the concepts in this book will help you grow and will encourage you to continually grow in leadership and in faith. As I sit here and write this conclusion, I already have ideas and words for more chapters to share with you in the future. Hopefully, a second book will be in order for those ideas.

I want to close this book with a few thoughts on growth and

learning in hopes that you use them to grow in your leadership. I want you to take the time to evaluate what you read and determine what areas you need to work on to better your leadership. Take notes and develop an action plan that you can follow to strengthen those areas. Develop a routine of growth. Set aside 10 to 15 minutes a day to grow in the areas you feel you need to develop. Once you have started to grow, then create a growth environment with your team and help them grow in the areas that they need growth. Growth helps develop people and people want to be developed because they want to succeed.

Rosalyn Carter said, "A leader takes people where they want to go. A great leader takes people where they don't necessarily want to go but ought to be." As a leader, you need to take your people where they "ought" to be. To do that, you have to help them grow and develop. But you also have to grow and develop yourself. You cannot lead growth and development if you are not willing to do so yourself.

John C. Maxwell once said, "People do not decide their future, they decide their habits and their habits decide their future." This statement is completely true and relates to growth. If you do not establish a growth "habit," you will not grow and in turn your future may not be as successful as you dreamed. Growth is a habit that you need to develop and use daily to keep yourself on track for a successful future.

Finally, John Powell said, "The only real mistake is the one from which we learn nothing." Always learn and grow. Do not make the mistake of not learning. We are never too old to learn. If you think you have reached an age that you cannot learn, then I advise you to get out of leadership. You can never stop learning as a leader. The leadership climate is always changing and you have to adjust your sails to stay ahead. If you stop learning, then you will sink in today's leadership climate.

I hope you were able to take at least one thing from this book that you feel you can learn from. I hope that you can use the lessons to strengthen yourself and those around you. I hope that you can share with others what you have learned and grow in your leadership. If you are able to do those things, then I feel that I have accomplished the goal of this book. The goal of helping leaders grow and develop.

Thank you for taking this time to include me in your leadership journey. I hope that I have written something that you can use in your daily leadership. Continue to grow and learn – that is all we can do as leaders. We can never stop learning. We can never stop growing. When we do, then I feel like this Afghan Proverb, "If you think you're leading and no one is following you, then you've only taken a walk." Stop learning and growing and then you will not be leading. You will be walking. God Bless your leadership journey!

REFERENCES

(1) Merriam-Webster Dictionary App, 2015.

(2) Merriam-Webster Dictionary App, 2015.

(3) Kevin Myers and John Maxwell, *Home Run* (New York: Faith Words, 2014).

(4) Merriam-Webster Dictionary App, 2015.

(5) Merriam-Webster Dictionary App, 2015.

(6) www.academy.com

(7) www.ge.com

(8) www.target.com

(9) John C. Maxwell, "Moses' Life Mission and His Five Big Excuses," *The Maxwell Leadership Bible* (Maxwell Motivation, Inc., and Thomas Nelson, Inc., 2nd Edition, 2007), 68.

(10) John C. Maxwell, *The Maxwell Leadership Bible* (Maxwell Motivation, Inc., and Thomas Nelson, Inc., 2nd Edition, 2007).

(11) John C. Maxwell, "The Law of Navigation," *The 21 Irrefutable Laws of Leadership* (Nashville, TN: Thomas Nelson, Inc., 1998), 33.

(12) John C. Maxwell, "The Law of the Big Mo," *The 21 Irrefutable Laws of Leadership* (Nashville, TN: Thomas Nelson, Inc., 1998), 165.

(13) John C. Maxwell, *Leadership Gold* (Nashville, TN: Thomas Nelson, Inc., 2008).

(14) Merriam-Webster Dictionary App, 2015.

(15) John C. Maxwell, "Gideon and the Law of Buy-In," *The Maxwell Leadership Bible* (Maxwell Motivation, Inc., and Thomas Nelson, Inc., 2nd Edition, 2007), 287.

(16) John C. Maxwell, "The Law of Influence," *The 21 Irrefutable Laws of Leadership* (Nashville, TN: Thomas Nelson, Inc., 1998), 11.

(17) John C. Maxwell, "The Law of Buy-In," *The 21 Irrefutable Laws of Leadership* (Nashville, TN: Thomas Nelson, Inc., 1998), 143.

(18) John C. Maxwell, *The Five Levels of Leadership* (New York: Center Street, 2011).

(19) John C. Maxwell, *The Maxwell Leadership Bible* (Maxwell Motivation, Inc., and Thomas Nelson, Inc., 2nd Edition, 2007).

(20) Merriam-Webster Dictionary App, 2015.

(21) Merriam-Webster Dictionary App, 2015.

(22) Merriam-Webster Dictionary App, 2015.

(23) Merriam-Webster Dictionary App, 2015.

(24) John C. Maxwell, "The Law of Sacrifice," *The 21 Irrefutable Laws of Leadership* (Nashville, TN: Thomas Nelson, Inc., 1998), 183.

(25) John C. Maxwell, "The Law of Sacrifice," *The 21 Irrefutable Laws of Leadership* (Nashville, TN: Thomas Nelson, Inc., 1998), 189.

(26) John C. Maxwell, *The Five Levels of Leadership* (New York: Center Street, 2011).

(27) Merriam-Webster Dictionary App, 2015.

ABOUT THE AUTHOR

Joshua Erin Elliott has been a student of leadership since his high school years. He actively studies leadership and teaches leadership to those on his team. He feels that you can never stop learning as a leader. He has now taken the next step, he feels, by writing about leadership. This is the first book he has written and hopes that many more will follow. His goal is to teach everyone he can about leadership. He wants to expand his reach outside of those on his team. He wants to add value to anyone who wants to listen. Currently, he is a Store Director for Academy Sports + Outdoors where he has been employed for over 9 years and teaches future leaders for the organization.

He is a 2001 graduate of W.S. Neal High School, a 2003 graduate of Jefferson Davis Community College, a 2005 graduate of The University of Alabama, and a 2007 graduate of The University of Alabama-Birmingham. You can follow him on Twitter using @JavyTimeJEE24.